WAYS OF BEING

ELEMENTS OF ANALYTIC ONTOLOGY

Woodbridge Lectures
Delivered at Columbia University
Number Seven

WAYS OF BEING

ELEMENTS OF ANALYTIC ONTOLOGY

HERBERT W. SCHNEIDER

COLUMBIA UNIVERSITY PRESS

NEW YORK AND LONDON 1962

WOODBRIDGE LECTURES

At his death in 1940 Professor Frederick Woodbridge left a bequest to Columbia University for the purpose of bringing distinguished philosophers to the University from time to time and for making their lectures available through publication. Some of Professor Woodbridge's friends made substantial additions to this bequest, and thus made it possible for the late President Butler to establish the Woodbridge Memorial Fund. The Woodbridge Lectures are delivered triennially. All these series have been published in book form by the Columbia University Press.

1. Wilmon H. Sheldon, *Process and Polarity*
2. George Plimpton Adams, *Man and Metaphysics*
3. Sterling Power Lamprecht, *Nature and History*
4. Harry Todd Costello, *A Philosophy of the Real and the Possible*
5. Clarence Irving Lewis, *The Ground and Nature of the Right*
6. William Ray Dennes, *Some Dilemmas of Naturalism*
7. Herbert W. Schneider, *Ways of Being: Elements of Analytic Ontology*

Library of Congress Catalog Card Number: 62-19907
Manufactured in the United States of America

INTRODUCTION

The importance of this work lies not in the work, though the labor has been long, but in the subject matter. When one surveys the beings of earth and sky, past and present, the visible and invisible, the intelligible and the unintelligible, the moving and the timeless, and then reflects on how the brightest stars in all their twinkling and how light itself on all its travels remain asleep, unimpressed by this overwhelming company, one begins to sense the privilege man has of being awake to so much of the world and of being able to wonder how much more may be going on unknown to him and how much more the past and future hold in store. One shrinks to speak above a whisper of "what there is" in the world and one does not dare to say "totality." One is tempted to stare at the incredible void and fulness in which man plays his little part. To orient himself, to make a useful map of the realms of being, seems a useless, impossible venture, especially now that the world, perhaps even the physical universe, is expanding at an explosive rate. The excitement of being awake in such a world makes it difficult to tell the plain truth. To be awake is problematic enough, but to try to tell in an orderly way how these sleeping beings all around us manage to be, and also how they have managed to bring man into being and into an awareness of being, this seems too fantastic a tale.

However, the attempt on man's part to orient himself in the world is as old as history, and apparently older. Each generation goes at it afresh, producing little of enduring worth, except that each generation has a little better sense of the magnitude of human ignorance. To conclude from all this that existence is meaningless would be evidently false; to hope that ontology may become a science seems wishful thinking.

Ontology is the investigation of what it means to be or not to be. Analytic ontology presupposes that there is a substantial body of information on what there is and what there is not, and it accepts such facts as its starting point in trying to determine what can be said about being in general. No science tries to do this, each is preoccupied with its particular instruments of search and field of vision; but together they provide reliable knowledge about many kinds of being. This makes it possible for ontology to take its modest place among the sciences, and without claiming to be a science, attempt to discover whether there can be a "science of being as being," to use the formula which has come down from Aristotle. What can be said about the ways in which various beings happen to be? And can this be said systematically without going beyond the limits of a factual inquiry?

Long before Descartes played with the so-called ontological argument as a mathematical toy, Aristotle had made a remarkable beginning in analysis by observing, instead of arguing, as follows:

> The varieties of essential being are indicated by the categories, for things may be said to be in as many ways as there are categories. Thus we say *what* there is, or what *kind* of being, or *how much,* or *how related,* or *how* it is *acting and reacting,* or *where* it is, or *when;* and these must all be ways of being.

> The question that has always been asked and is still being asked today, the ever-puzzling question, "What is being?" amounts to this: "What being is primary?" Some say unified being, others say diversified being; some say finite, others say infinite. . . . Primary being is thought to belong most evidently to bodies; as illustrations we point to animals, plants, or their parts, also to fire, water, earth, and the like, or their elements and compounds, or to the heavens, stars, sun and moon. . . . But some hold that the surfaces of bodies, their planes, lines, and points are more primary than their solid substance. Others think that only sense-objects are primary. Still others think that there are eternal beings, more in number and of finer nature than sense objects.[1]

This search for the primary way of being led Aristotle into what some have called his ousiology. He subordinated the doctrine of ontological categories to the doctrine that of all the categories the primary one, the one that came closest to telling the peculiar "thisness" of any being as being, is the category that tells "what" it means to be that particular individual being.

I do not wish to begin with a critique of Aristotle, but I call attention to the way in which he shifted the problem of the

---

[1] Aristotle, *Metaphysics* 1017a, 1028b. Richard Hope translation (New York; Columbia University Press, 1952).

"how" of being to the "what" of being. This shift turned out to be fateful, for few of his followers have turned back to the "how." Few have recovered Aristotle's initial concern with the verb "to be" but have taken for granted that the primary problem is to find out "what" it means to be a being (being as a noun). A renewed concern with the verb "to be" has come as a result of the existentialist concentration on human existence. It has been a commonly held doctrine in both East and West that man is to be conceived in terms of his toil and suffering, his cares and anxieties, and that his natural being is "brutish, nasty and short." Such doctrines called attention to "how" man is, and his behavior during the twentieth century has reenforced them. This preoccupation with human existence has crowded out of interest the more general aspects of being; but gradually a so-called "fundamental ontology" is making its way, emerging in dreadful shape from attempts to conceive the world as man's world and to understand all things as they enter into human existence.

Hence we have before us the delicate operation of keeping alive the existentialist interest in the "how" of being while cutting out its anthropocentric methods of analysis. There is no reason why we should begin our inquiry with the being that is peculiar to man. We do not know our own being any better than we know that of inanimate objects or of hydrogen atoms, or of numbers, or of reasoning. The science of man is extremely difficult and the human being is the most complicated kind of being we know about. It would seem prudent, therefore, to begin with other entities in the world about us. The world is not man's world; this we now know, for he appropriates it with difficulties and risks. Man knows that his situation involves his relations to many other beings and that a more objective study of how these other beings exist or "be" may serve to give man a more accurate perspective on his own type of being than he can get by relying on the pretended "open" road of existentialist analysis. However, the existentialists have taken a promising road by their reinterpretation of being as an engagement in and to a situation, either historical or natural. Such a method of analysis brings ontology closer to the natural and social sciences.

The analysis or orientation that follows is intended to rest on the elementary information gathered about the world by the various sciences. It makes no new contributions to this information. Its aim is to put things of all sorts into some kind of order; it is primarily a filing away of individual beings according to their proper fields of being. There is no map of the world as a whole, no cosmology, for there is no science of the whole world and I have been unable to find a privileged place where I could get a panoramic view of the world from the outside. I have done the best I could to describe as much as I could from the inside, where the view is not too good.

What virtue the work may have is as a book of orientation or reference, in which things appear to be where they really belong to be. I have used my little system for about twenty years, with minor repairs, and all I can say is what country auctioneers say about the old washing machines they try to sell: "The last time I used it, it was in running order." Philosophical systems, like washing machines, have a way of becoming antiques before they wear out. New times bring new devices. From my particular point of vantage this system appears to me to have borrowed good points from many models, especially those of Aristotle, Hobbes, Santayana, and Peirce; and it is certainly indebted to my teachers Woodbridge and Dewey. But the scheme as a whole I have worked out for myself, with the help of many students and the advice of many friends. I find it useful, and truthful. Others may not have much luck with it and will probably work out something more like their own world.

Meanwhile, the world is changing and there may be objective reasons why ontology needs to be revised and rewritten. This I present for today only as an elementary formulation of what it now means to be in the world as it now is.

H. W. S.

Claremont, California
June, 1962

CONTENTS

I. LOGIC AND ONTOLOGIC

The logicians have stumbled into ontology with the question, "What *is* there?" It has been forced on them in consequence of their difficulties with another question, "What is an individual?" This is a logical question, but "logical individuals" have a way of hiding behind metaphysical screens. The traditional *principium individuationis* gets in the way of the strictly logical question. In their effort to free themselves from such traditional nuisances, the logicians replied that they needed no "principle" here; for them, an individual could be recognized without credentials as simply "whatever happens to be." But this simple doctrine landed the logicians squarely among the ontologists, who were struggling with the question of whether or not it happens to be the case that only individuals are. They found themselves in a situation similar to that of Carlyle, who, after studying the problem of "action-at-a-distance," concluded with: "I am quite willing to admit that things can't act where they aren't, but I'd like to know, where in the world *are* they?" How to locate an individual, that is the question. When Adam and Eve after their fall heard their Creator ask his first question of them, "Where are you now?" they answered with more ontological analysis than most of their descendents can command: "We are naked in the bushes, ashamed, and must work for a living." Such a three-dimensional answer to a simple "Where?" might have a sobering effect on us, when we ask glibly, "Where is anything?" The logicians, warned of the fallacy of "simple location," insist on postponing the "where?" until the "what?" has been settled. First, "What" is there? Whose question deserves priority, God's "where?" or the logician's "what?"? Both appear to be at "the beginning." Perhaps they can be answered jointly?

CATEGORICAL QUESTIONS

These questions belong to a small group of elemental questions which are being asked continually without being answered generally. "How are you?" is repeated constantly, but is seldom interpreted as a question. Nevertheless, it suggests, "How is anything?" In addition to "what, where, and how?" we are continually confronted with "why, who, which, when, whence, whither, wherefor, whereof, wherein, wherewithal?" but the list of these questions is not long. They are all contained in a few verses of Omar Khayyam:

> I came like water, and like wind I go
> Into this universe, and *why* not knowing
> Nor *whence,* like water willy-nilly flowing;
> And out of it, as wind along the waste,
> I know not *whither,* willy-nilly blowing.
>
> *What,* without asking, *hither* hurried *whence?*
> And, without asking, *whither* hurried *hence.*

"Without asking" such questions, we manage to make our way in the world, but when we stop to ask, there is endless trouble of spirit. These are the questions children ask, and only fools, ontologists, and logicians attempt to explain. Let us call them categorical questions. They are usually casual and, when referred to a particular being, not very difficult. But if they must be generalized, can they be systematized, or must we leave them in this haphazard lack of order?

Aristotle, who first studied this matter, thought the most elemental of all is "why?" because included in any complete answer to "why?" were four of the others: "what" is it? "whereof" is it? "whence" came it? and "wherefor" is it? Without engaging in a criticism of this classic scheme, let me suggest another, not because it is better, but because it seems to me to correspond more closely to the way things are today. We must not forget, we ontologists and logicians, that times have changed since Aristotle's day, and it seems highly probable that things are not today in just the same way they were when he first looked into them.

I agree with Aristotle that there are four basic questions here, but they are not his four, and they begin with "how?" rather than with "why?". I would place first under "how?" questions like "who?" or "which?" They call for *identification* of beings. They usually get pointings or pointers as answers: this, that, the other one. And if pointing is impractical, they call for terms of reference: names, telephone numbers, street addresses, card catalogue numbers, points on a map, or lines on a chart or scale.

These answers do not tell us "what" there is; merely "that" there is something here or there, now or then. Such ontological reference or identification has nothing to do with mathematical statements of identity. For a mathematical logician it is important to postulate that if there is A, then A is A. But, of course, A would be A, even if there were no A. So self-identity, which is a logical relation, is quite different from being identifiable. An identifiable something carries with it, in case it should meet a logician, an existential quantifier which makes of it a "bound variable" and enables the logician to state "It is the case that . . ." When thus identified or referred to, it becomes a fit candidate for the subject of an existential proposition, and its proper name is treated with all the respect due to a bona fide "case." Thus a thing identified or tagged as an accredited entity becomes a potential subject of discourse, and the logician, or any less qualified person for that matter, may proceed to tell us "what" the thing is by treating it with predicates as a case. But merely as identified, before it gets stated in a proposition, it is a bare "that" or "this," a "he who" or an "it which." It is commonly known among logicians as a singular; known, that is, in the sense of "recognized as being" by its name or number. For logic, the fewer there are of these singular nuisances the better; propositions are more readily formulated in terms of free variables.

This takes me to the second type of categorical question, the "what?" Answers to this question place the identified entity within a class, group, genus, type, or some other device for fencing it in. The individual then becomes a genuine "instance." The question, "What is it?" calls for description, definition, qualification, predication. First of all, the logician or scientist would like to know from whoever happens to know the facts of the case, whether the identified "that" is a thing, an event, a relation, a quality, a universal, an abstraction, a fact, or whatever other basic classes of beings may be generally recognized by them. If it should be an abstraction, for instance, it would be assigned by the more cautious among the logicians to a limbo or vestibule or purgatory for better identification before it could be admitted to be. The "what" of an accredited entity need not be restricted to its typological classification or definition; any property or dispositional predicate contributes something to the "what" of an entity. But ideally we do not claim to know "just what" anything is until we can describe what-it-means-to-be-that-thing. When such a "what" is known, our categorical question gets a categorical answer, and the "that" gets definitely located in the logician's filing cabinet. When things are properly filed or located systematically, the logician can begin his operations, and not until then; for he must be able to *say* what things are in an orderly fashion, and not go around pointing here and there with proper names, or smelling distinctions like a dog.

A third group of questions is : "why," "where," "whence," "wherefor," "whereof," "whereto?." These seek to *correlate* individual beings with other individual beings, whether they are of the same kind of being or of different kinds. The kinds

or classes themselves need to be correlated. The network of
relations which connect all kinds of beings with each other
includes causal relations, logical relations, coincidences, uses,
measurement, and many others. Relations themselves must be
correlated. By means of these diversified systems of correlation
it is possible to explain "why" beings do what they do in a
variety of contexts and perspectives.

A fourth group of elemental questions centers about the
question, "wherein". "To be" means more than to be in the
world; it means to belong in a context, field, situation, or frame
of being. Different things have different environments or
natural habitats. To know "wherein" a being moves "and has
its being" means to specify the being's situation. Membership
in an ontological field or environment or context is quite distinct
from membership in a group or class of beings, though a
group may share an ontological domain or world-region. The
"wherein" locates an individual in terms of its proper functioning as a being inherently rooted or situated in a field, as distinguished from location by correlation with its neighbors, or
status in terms of logical definition. Such a field or realm
of being is not a cognitive creation but an actual situation or
residence for beings. In the universe of discourse or logic things
are uprooted from their proper habitats in the world and given
new neighbors and diverse relations. *Orientation,* then, is orientation in the world, not in a formal system of reference or
language.

Taken together, these categorical questions all ask "how" a

being manages to be. A way of being, in short, is explained by four intellectual operations: identification, definition, correlation, and orientation. It will be evident at once that these four operations are basic to logic as well as to ontologic. These are categories of reason as well as of being. Our problem, then, is to explain the differences between the logical and the ontological use of these four operations.

ONTOLOGIC

The most general difference between logic and ontologic is that logic is not concerned directly with how things are, but with how "we can say" they are. Logic is formulation, and formulation for purposes of communication. By logic the world is transposed into propositions, and beings into parts of speech. Logic itself is an operation upon the world. There would be no logic if there were nothing to say or measure. It is the case that there were events long before they became "cases," and there were things long before there were instances. For logic, identification is the art of pointing symbolically to that about which an assertion or a question or an evaluation is to be made. In identifying or referring to a something, logic transposes the something into a subject. Ontology, too, must use language and logical forms; it should become a respectable science among the sciences. Hence its first and most delicate task is to say what being is like before being is said to be what it is. This is ontologic's first predicament: how to describe undescribed being, how to report a being as it really is and not as it is said to be.

Both logic and ontologic share the awareness that they must deal fairly with individuals, but they have different ideals of fairness. In logic the operations of identification and orientation are subordinated to the operations of definition and correlation; whereas in ontologic the operations of identification and orientation are primary. In logic, "what" and "why" are uppermost concerns; in ontologic, "that," "where," and "how." Logic prepares things for the operating rooms of laboratories; ontologic must somehow restore the patients to their homes. Logically nothing can be recognized as an individual without putting "an individual" into the predicate. "So-and-so is an individual." means that "individual" is a property or class name attributed to a being. It is "what" the subject is said to be. But individuals like us, for example, must be identified ontologically not as belonging to the class of individuals but simply as having their proper places in the world. In logic a proper name is a surd, for it says nothing. Anything as such is a logical surd, but it is precisely with these surds that ontologic must somehow deal. The logician cannot use "existence" or "existent" as a predicate. The ontologist tries to get around this difficulty by using "existing" as a verb. The logician must regard "So-and-so is" as an incomplete sentence; So-and-so must be said to be "something." But the ontologist insists that when there is something to be said, that something is a thing-in-being before it is "what" is said of it. This ancient dialectic seems hopeless as well as useless. But how evade it?

The same kind of puzzle confronts us if, instead of examining

the relation of identification to logical definition and to ontological orientation, we turn to correlation. Bradley's paradox of
terms and relations is too familiar to need rehearsal here. Suffice
it to note that this paradox is but an instance of the more general
misunderstanding that results when logical and ontological
orientations are confused. If beings are individuals, so the argument runs, they are themselves and exist in self-identity. If
they are related, the relation has its own being and the terms
to be related become mere instances of a relation. Terms of a
relation are then not beings in their own right. How can both
terms and relations be? If they are all one, then nothing is anything. Therefore things cannot possibly exist as they are said
to be when correlated. Relations and correlations are logical
stock in trade; but they make the being of things unintelligible.
It is evident that any logical term exists in the universe of
discourse. It is there that it is at home. If a term is not an item
of discourse, it is meaningless and hence homeless. Where in
the world can it be? If it cannot be found in the universe of
discourse, it cannot be found anywhere, for there is no more
inclusive world than the world of talk. This is a variation on the
theme that a naked "that" must be clothed in a "what" before
it is fit for recognition in any science, including ontology.

What shall we say about this ancient dialectic, which keeps
logician and ontologist at odds? My only suggestion, and it
may be acceptable to neither party, is that the verb "to be"
cannot be made intelligible in terms of any one operation:
neither by mere identification of beings, nor by saying "what"

there is, nor by correlating beings as if objective relativism were the whole truth, nor by contextual orientation. Only the combination of all four operations is adequate for explaining "how" anything is. And this holds for both logic and ontologic. These four factors of categorical analysis represent four directions of inquiry which are all necessary before a logician can say all there is or an ontologist can explain how all things are. This requires that logicians must be ready to give "to be" a different meaning for different types of beings, and that ontologists must explain accurately how beings differ categorically. In other words, if what-it-means-to-be has no single definition, and how things are has no single explanation, both logic and ontologic become more complicated than they are supposed to be. It may be necessary to have several kinds of existential quantifiers in logic, if ontology finds that things have different ways of being. A factual critique of the *a priori* doctrine that being is necessarily "one" may save both logicians and ontologists from tearing out their own and each others' hair. The ontologist could then admit that things are "what" they are indeed; provided the logician will admit that this "what" is not *all* they are, for they are also "where" and "how" they are.

THE ONTOLOGICAL ARGUMENT

But something more is needed before logic and ontologic can peacefully go each its own way. The traditional ontological argument must be abandoned. The essence of this argument is the attempt to give a deductive form or "grounding" to the science of being. The variations on this attempt are different arguments for transforming logical certainty into ontological evidence or formal reason into existential subject matter. There should be, so they say, some way of showing that being *must* be. It is too naïve to take being for granted as given factually and as open for investigation. Being may be hiding behind appearances, or may be beyond man's grasp, or may be too near to be observed. There are many such possibilities. Before ontology can go its analytic way there must be some proof, according to traditional conceptions of "grounding," that it is a possible science among sciences. Being would seem to most laymen to be as near rock-bottom as one could expect to get, but the ontological experts insist that ontological truth must be necessary truth, otherwise the foundation of all facts is itself without foundation, which is absurd.

I shall take note of only two of the many versions of this argument. The briefest and best, so it seems to me, is contained in Aristotle's *Metaphysics*. Aristotle was content to admit that not all being is necessary. Some kinds of being and some particular beings might well not be; they exist contingently. But, reasoned he, there must be something which necessarily is, otherwise it would be the case that being might disappear entirely; "which is absurd." It may be absurd, but I fail to see why it is impossible. This may be the case, for all we know. For this proposition, that nothing is necessary, is neither nonsense nor self-contradictory; it may be unverifiable and it may be foolish. Apparently, Aristotle's Greek for "absurdity" was as ambiguous as is our contemporary usage. Many absurd things happen and more absurd things are said, and said logically enough. It might seem absurd to us, if we knew that at such and such a time all being would come to an end, but absurd endings are not unheard of. We can be without having the security or comfort of knowing that not all can perish. Even on this insecure footing, which is no worse than that of other sciences, ontology can proceed. To provide logical terra firma for ontology is to concoct sugar pills for timid souls. Even in mathematics there are discoveries to the effect that "this-is-how-it-is." Why should not ontology accept whatever there is with all its absurdities?

Being is bound to be a logical surd; it is always more than we say it is. There is always an existential remainder. The "existential quantifier" is formal logic's formal bow to the ontological surd. But it is absurd to call the world absurd merely because there are such surds in it. To call fact "brute fact" is not very polite; it reflects an emotional attitude, just as it is emotional expression to say that whatever is is right, or that *ens et bonum convertuntur*. Such ontological attributes are human inventions, not ontological data.

René Descartes, whom it is fashionable to dismiss "respectfully" and to whom, we, too, must make our bow, gave a new twist to ontological logic. He argued that it is logically certain that there are at least two beings: René Descartes and a perfect being. From their existence all the rest could be deduced. Descartes, the thinking Descartes, or at least the doubter, was compelled to admit that his existence was indubitable. And he challenged any other doubter to doubt himself. "I wonder whether or not I exist," *ergo* I exist. How do I exist? As a wonderer. If we take the *ergo* seriously in this argument, we must admit that there is an implicit major premise here: Only beings can wonder. Now this proposition is not self-evident and rests on empirical generalization. Or it rests on the still more general empirical proposition that only beings can do anything. This might be a postulate, to be sure, but it needs empirical justification. When such implications of the *ergo* in his famous *cogito* were called to his attention, Descartes replied promptly that the *ergo* is not essential to the argument. No syllogism is intended here. *Cogito sum* is a single, intuitive fact. Self-existence is self-evident, he thought. But he might sooner have done without the *ego* than without the *ergo*. He might have said, *cogitans sum,* which might be rendered into English as, "I am involved in a process of thinking" or *cogitatio est*. "There is thinking and I am in it." Here the thinker is less certain than the thinking process, and it might take considerable psychology to show that thinking requires a thinker. If Descartes really wished to raise the question of agency, that is, of who or what does the thinking, he certainly involved himself in a complicated factual analysis. And if he took the act of *saying* "cogito" seriously, he was implying the fact of communication, which in turn implies a "we" and mouth and ears and at least a bit of brains behind the saying and hearing.

In short, I do not believe that the *cogito sum* intuition can be defended as a logical proof that "a thinking being" must exist. The certainty presumably contained in this self-evident situation is really derived from the more general proposition about action and being, which is not logically certain. If I were to say, "I am saying," you would wait for me to say something and would not regard it as a complete sentence. If I stopped still shorter and said merely, "I am," you might have even more ground for thinking, "Go on with the sentence." If in reply I were to insist that when I am saying, "There is something doing," and analogously also when I am being, it should be possible to specify "what" is doing when something is being said or when something is being. And this seems to me to raise a genuine ontological problem, not the old ontological argument.

As for Descartes' second argument: "I have an idea of a perfect being, which, to be perfect, must at least exist, and therefore does exist," it might appear that this argument is analogous to the evident truth that "The tallest living man must exist." If "great," "greater," and "greatest" beings could be lined up on a scale, as men would be for the measuring of their heights, there might be a point to the assertion. But Descartes does not suggest such a scale for greatness and does not define degrees of perfection. He claims simply to have "an idea" of the greatest possible being. This claim can well be doubted. I for one am convinced that his phrase "perfect being" is merely verbal and contains no idea at all. For there is nothing in the idea of being to give concrete meaning to "perfection of being." Whether perfect being is extended or not, infinite or not, just or not, substantial or not, present or past or future, are all questions which reflect *human* conceptions of perfection in contexts less general than "being." I am inclined to think that Descartes had no genuine idea of "perfection" at all, and possibly not of "being."

So much for logical sheep dressed in ontological wolf fur. Such arguments commit neither logicians nor ontologists to anything. The genuine ontological commitments of logic we have already discussed, and the logical commitments of ontology are none other than those of any other concrete scientific analysis.

THE ONTOLOGICAL EXCLUDED MIDDLE

There is, however, one other logical trap into which ontologic is apt to fall. A logician is apt to expect an ontologist to admit that A either is or is not, as if this proposition were of the form p or non-p, a pair of contradictories. But ontologically it is not necessary to assume that anything either is or is not. It may be becoming. It may be in one way and not in another. It may be past and yet not not-be. It may be absent and yet be. It may be possible, which makes it neither a being or a non-being. Being and non-being are not logical opposites. They constitute an ontological pair, whose precise relations are difficult to determine; in any case, the relations must be determined ontologically and not merely logically.

Finally, there is a semantic absurdity into which ontologists fall too easily, and of which I may have been guilty myself in an off moment. To use expressions like "being is," "the being of non-being," "the being of being," obviously involve the user in semantic embarrassments, which are often interpreted as profound paradoxes or ontological *aporia*. The pseudo-problems which can be thus generated are only too familiar. It is not always easy to evade these traps, but they are not confined to ontological syntax. They can usually be detected wherever there are *meta*-troubles. Let us be on our guard. Ontological syntax is difficult, but it need not be nonsense. Nor need such puzzles be formalized as if ontology were a deductive system. Let ontology use what language it needs, so long as it uses it to report the facts and not to obscure them. Whenever ontology gets speculative and rhetorical the time has come to call in the logicians' fire engines to put the fire out. Meanwhile, not all ontology is fit for burning.

INDIVIDUALITY

Traditional ontology has engaged in the search for a *principium individuationis*. Some theorists have maintained that the form or shape is the source of individual being; others have defended matter as such a source, since unembodied forms are universal, not concrete. Aristotle cut this Gordian knot in advance by defining an individual as a synthesis of matter and form, a *synholon,* which the Scholastics translated into a substance, substances being distinguished from *substantia* without a plural. This synthetic idea of individuality has come down in classical tradition as the doctrine that an individual is a concretion or a concreted universal. In contemporary idioms an individual is usually identified as an "instance" or "case" of a class or function. Against this whole tradition I shall try to defend individuality as a category of ontological analysis; individuals are not formed by uniting un-individuated elements, for they are themselves ultimate elements of being.

Being is individuated. This fact cannot be explained by any of the creation myths which represent individuals as products of a process of concretion. There is a persistent doctrine that "in the beginning" there was homogeneity, flux, ocean of being, cosmic womb or egg, whence issued individuals. There is supposed to be a creative process of emergent evolution which culminates in individuated beings. Or there is still "In the Beginning" the creative Word which decides, "Let there be this and that." To be sure, individuals come into being or become, some of them quite slowly. But such becoming is a process of transformation, from individual unto individual; likewise, the perishing of one individual is the creation of another. Unindividuated being is an abstraction or a mythical monster for which there is no evidence. It is more reasonable to accept individuality as a basic fact, than to invent stories about its origin.

Prominent among contemporary ontologists who still refuse to accept individuated being as an ultimate datum is Martin Heidegger, who claims that it is logically retrogressive to begin with beings (*Seiendes*) in order to understand Being. Being must be known before beings become intelligible, because beings do not form a class or genus. The world is not a genuine collection or aggregate of beings; "world" is not a collective term. And "being" is still less a collective or class name for beings. "Speaking" might represent collectively all acts of speech, and since one cannot speak without using a particular language or algebra, all speaking is a "speaking in tongues" and hence essentially pluralistic. Analogously, a superficial ontologist, says Heidegger, might argue that because it is impossible to be without being something in particular, knowledge of being, as of speaking, must rise from the particulars to the universal. But the case of being is unique, Heidegger insists; Being is not the *summum genus* of beings. A *summum* is logical, not ontological; so is also "genus." Even if "the class of beings" were not a meaningless collection, it would not be equivalent to what "being" means. Admitting this much of Heidegger's methodology, we need not follow him in trying to get a "grounding" or foundation for being elsewhere than in beings. If being is not terra firma, it is not being; for what could be more basic? Being is a verb; it means the way or ways beings be. If there are no modes of being, there would be little use for ontology. Heidegger agrees with practically all ontologists that there are modes. But he will not begin with modes anymore than with individuals. He must be able to say what the modes are modes of. Let us be less ambitious. Let us begin with the modes and look for actual types of being and kinds of beings, whatever being-in-general may turn out to be. Heidegger's brave attempts to explain Being as Being regardless of beings, by a kind of ontological skin-diving, brings him up from the deeps with such discoveries as that "Being is grounded in its own freedom." This may be a revelation, but a mere ontologist can get out of it even less than he can get out of the fishing among particular beings. In any case, let us no longer postpone an examination of individuals without further foundation than the bottomless ocean of being.

To begin with things—*in medias res*. We are told that the "thing language" is antiquated, ambiguous, unscientific, expendable. Carnap tells us that the reference to things means nothing except reliance on the "thing language." For all we know, there are no things, they say, and we can improve our conventional language by substituting more precise terms. Call them "events" or "routes of occasions" or Eφχ, but make no existential commitments to things. I have tried repeatedly to follow this advice conscientiously, but in the end I find myself stumbling onto things. They get in the way as if they were real. I think the current prejudice against their existence stems less from the clumsiness of the "thing language" than from two epistemological embarrassments. (1) The reference to "things-in-themselves" or "things-per-se" has proved a disaster. But the trouble comes not from the "thing language" but from the "per se". That things exist in themselves is a gratuitous assumption, as philosophers still delight in showing. But if we admit that anything is related to something or other and that relationality is a fact of being generally, we are more than ready to dispense with things-in-themselves. We might even surrender things *an-und-für-sich* as well as the *en-soi* and the *pour-soi*. We can get along in our thing language with beings among each other and among us. And we can postpone the difficult decision whether or not we shall call ourselves things.

(2) Things are apt to be pointed at or to have proper names and this causes logical trouble. According to Bertrand Russell, it is correct to say "The author of Waverly existed," but not correct to say that "Sir Walter Scott existed." "So-and-so exists" is not a complete sentence, whereas it makes sense to say, "There is an entity such that, etc." Such a theory of descriptions may solve a semantic difficulty, but it makes little difference to ontologic. Let things be entities if they must!

I recall a notable "qualitied event" that took place some years ago at Columbia University, room 307 Philosophy Hall. Bertrand Russell delivered his famous "penny lecture" in which he explained to us how the "round penny" which he exhibited to us had to be constructed by a complicated correlation of optical perspectives out of a group of elliptical sense-data. After the lecture Woodbridge commented, "You noticed that he put the real thing in his pocket." It is quite true that a penny does not exist in itself. Its relations to lecturers, observers, pockets, shillings, pounds, dollars, newspapers, are all in a penny's day. To have such a variegated environment is an essential aspect of its being. But in all these complications, the thing is still a thing among others, even if the others are mere sense-data. No single relation is constitutive of a penny's existence, even if it has an essence, and no penny would be anything in and by itself.

Now we come to things that we hesitate to call things or individuals, what Quine calls "bulk objects" (earth, air, fire, water). These objects seem to exist in-bulk as if they could exist in-themselves if they had to. Oceans, flames, mountain ranges, atmospheres are things in certain contexts, and in others they bulk so large as to be themselves contexts. A brick in a brick-yard and a liver in a butcher-shop are more individual than are a brick-in-the-wall and a liver-in-an-organism. Individuality is not only relational but relative. A wall loses its individuality when the building is completed. A building is absorbed into a university and the university into a city. Cities are individuals among cities and in landscapes, but both cities and landscapes enter into the individuality of a country, a continent, the earth, or the solar system. Similarly, molecules, atoms, electrons, quanta, photons, emerge in certain laboratory contexts as things whose individual behavior is studied intensively, whereas in the macroscopic contexts they exist "in bodies" rather than as bodies, or, perhaps, as Bridgman argued, they exist only in certain machines and experiments.

Not all things are physical bodies. Among the things mentioned above, universities, cities, and countries are "bodies politic" as well as collections of physical things. Bodies are a type of individual beings, but there is individuality among beings that are not things—among relations, qualities, events, characters, numbers, compositions, sciences and arts—the list is long. It is not very important where we draw the line between things and other types of individuals. Sometimes we refer to pains, sunrises, business affairs, conspiracies, intentions, as things; whereas we seldom think of revolution, institutions, theories, friendships as things, though they have individuality. It is useful to leave "thing" as ambiguous and useful as the Latin *res*.

We ought to be a bit more definite in our notions about individuals. Otis Lee, who tried to make a precise definition, spoke of an individual as "a concrete entity" and then defined this term as "any existent with a structure and component energies and powers, so related that the entity is and behaves as a unit. It is not only unique but it is unique in a certain way."[1] "Concrete" has the objectionable implications to which I have referred. Not all individuals have "energies"; some "behave" only in symbolical systems. I think "unity" would be better than "unit" and "uniqueness" seems to me not an essential attribute. A postage stamp on a letter is an individual. Like any other individual it may be called "unique" in the sense that there is no other stamp which is this stamp, but there are millions of other stamps "just like it." It is a "unit" on a sheet of stamps, but it is a unity on a letter. Though it may have little or no qualitative uniqueness, it is an individual by virtue of its unique function in a specific message.

1 Otis Lee, *Existence and Inquiry* (Chicago; University of Chicago Press, 1949), p. 303.

As an adjective, "individual" is more precise than as a noun. Individuality is more categorical than the class of individuals or things. It is careless to name individuals in isolation as though they constituted a class of entities when mentioned collectively. But admitting these limitations of the use of the noun, it is necessary to have an ontological term for a basic trait of being— for *Seiendes*. Without discussing the whole range of categories we need to make sure of individuation first.

Individuals are commonly said to have the peculiar kind of being called "existence." Hence, a few words about existence. An existence is outstanding, eminent in its context, though not necessarily among its fellow individuals. An individual emerges from its context by its unified behavior. Cicero, who seems to have invented *existere*, or at least to have first made it important for ontology, used it to denote beings that were external and objective, not of human beings; whereas the existentialists of today or yesterday use "existence" largely to denote the human way of being. In either case "existence" is applied to a specialized type of being. Among the British philosophers of today existences are much less outstanding; almost anything in nature or experience will pass as an existence. There are numbers but they do not exist. Relations do not exist themselves but serve to connect existences. Ideas, which are treated very respectfully on the Continent, are not said to exist within the British Isles.

The confusion in terminology is due in part to the difficulty of distinguishing between individual beings and logical particulars or simples. There might be less confusion if individuation were recognized as a trait of all kinds of beings and therefore as a category, and if individuals were not limited to things nor to persons. The adjectival use of "individual" is less apt to cause confusion, provided that the relativity of individuality as a quality is admitted. Within a given context, the definition of an individual being in that context should not be too difficult. An individual could well be said to be existent within its field, standing out from it, emerging from its field or matrix *in* which it nevertheless is "grounded." The correlative of an existent or individual being would then be its field or context, and by its field it would be known to be a certain kind of individual. It is the fields that are individuated; but they are not individuals. What the several categorial fields are to each other I cannot say—at least, not yet.

II. NATURAL BEING

BASIC BEING

Woodbridge lectures naturally begin with nature, but even were I free it would seem proper to me to begin the analysis where beings begin. It appears to be useless and perhaps impossible to justify this approach but since it is an unconventional starting point for ontology, I owe it to you, if not to Woodbridge, to make the attempt.

A human being is naturally circumspect and extravert, attracted physically by what goes on about him; but philosophers for some inhuman reason stand on their heads to look at the world and begin their analysis with philosophical being, where I propose to end. However, my reason for beginning with the natural way of being is not a humanist reason; rather, I ought to make clear, if anyone doubts it, that nature is basic, foundational for being itself. Natural being presupposes no other kind and serves as the dynamic matrix and source of all that moves. Nature, as the word suggests, is self-starting, automobile, the generator of generators. Its processes and their fields have characteristic structures, but what the nature of nature as a whole is, no man knows.

Sir James Jeans, commenting on Galileo's saying that "Nature's great book is written in mathematical language," claims that only a mathematician can ever "unravel the funda- mental nature of the universe."[1] It may well be that natural processes and causes can be expressed only by mathematical equations, but mathematics is no longer an "unraveling," now that mathematicians can find formulae for any chaos. A mathe- matical unraveling is none too fundamental, since it too needs interpretation into something less than symbols and mysteries. After all, a great book ought to be readable, or it ought at least to indicate which mathematics is fundamental. I have been restudying Spinoza, who thought he could read nature's book and put it into Latin geometrically. I would agree with him that the order of nature may exist per se, but I do not believe that it can be conceived per se. It can be conceived as funda- mental for other ways of being, but its own foundations seem inconceivable. In any case, nature *is* more than pure mathemat- ics. It is not only the dynamic matrix or "ocean of being" whence particular beings emerge, but it remains the container or "receptacle" *within* which all events happen and all that moves has its being. There are orders in and of nature, but it seems impossible for nature to be nothing but an order, pure food for pure mathematicians. So let nature be identified, at

---

[1] Sir James Jeans, *The Mysterious Universe* (Cambridge; Cambridge Uni- versity Press, 1930) p. 112.

least provisionally, as "the amorphous totality of genuinely elemental processes."[2]

NATURAL FIELDS

Every natural being has a compound orientation. No one form of measurement or location exhausts its structure and power. Though all things are encompassed in nature's domain, they are not wholly united, preserved, or destroyed by any one process, or confined in one field. They are multidimensional; they may occur in assignable places and moments, but within a very complex frame of reference.

This frame of reference or orientation in nature is composed of several fields or dynamic contexts within which things in process are conditioned. They may be termed the modes of natural conditioning. They are not as distinct as systematic ontologies represent them to be. They do not constitute a single cosmos or order of nature, neither are they individual beings in nature; they are *of* nature, not *in* it. It would be meaningless to assert that they condition each other, for each is a basic conditioner of individual processes; nevertheless, they are together in an indefinable way, overlapping in their functioning since they jointly provide the context for processes. Such conditioning which provides the natural habitats for all that moves must be clearly distinguished from the causal relations among natural beings. It is not an agent in the processes

---

2 Paul Schrecker, *Work and History* (Princeton; Princeton University Press, 1948) p. 309.

of interaction among bodies, but merely the domain, neighborhood, or "residence" (to use the more anthropomorphic term employed by some ontologists) within which causation takes place. Together they provide at least the outline of an answer to what it means to be "in nature" and to the problem of complex orientation or location. But they leave the meaning of *in* unexplained and suggest that even the world in which we move, to say nothing of other ways of "having our being" is a complicated "receptacle."

NATURAL PROCESSES

The identification of natural individuals is equally complicated. The idea of a "world process" or universal evolution still haunts many philosophical and scientific imaginations. But the progress of the natural sciences and their plurality afford slight evidence for this faith. The Greek idea of *physis,* the principle of natural realization of potentialities followed by decline and perishing, is evidently a generalization based on organic beings. Though it has served as a classic model for the concept of all natural processes, it is too biological to apply to all. The other Greek idea, that natural processes are the struggles of opposites, polar or dialectical, is also too narrow a model. Cyclical or "perfect" motion in endless orbits, however perfect it may be, is not universal. *Physis* is correlated in Greek with *poiēsis* and expresses the contrast between natural doings and artful makings, between causation and creation. I shall criticize this sharp distinction as I go along, and attempt to include certain types of

production or making as natural. On the other hand, to interpret the natural processes as the creation or art of a supernatural
creator is ruinous for a critical conception of the difference
between nature and culture. Nature is not art.

There are several types of processes, at least as many as there
are natural sciences. It may be possible to distinguish certain
types which will serve to identify the basic relational structures
among natural bodies and processes. Such types of natural
relatedness are usually identified as types of causation, and
types of causation are identified in terms of types of explanation. Though these distinctions of science are related to our
ontological classification, I shall discuss them not as types of
explanation or correlation but as types of natural being, taking
for granted that because there are these varieties of natural
being, there are various natural sciences and methods of inquiry.
However, it cannot be taken for granted that these types
correspond to the conventional divisions among the natural
sciences. Each science is concerned with more than one type,
though it specializes on certain aspects of nature.

LOCATION IN SPACE-TIME

I shall try to mention the various modes in the order of
generality, though such an order cannot be defined exactly.
Roughly, this order indicates advance from the most inclusive
orientation in nature to the kinds of conditioning that apply to
specialized types of natural things and processes. I distinguish
five categorial fields.

The first and most general field is the space-time continuum, or the four-dimensional continuum. This continuum no more exists *in* nature than do the basic beings of classical ontology, space and time. It is a dimension of nature, the most universal domain of all that moves. In it take place all successions of events, all concatenations, all simultaneities, all movements that can be measured physically. Some say it is composed of cosmic points. This I doubt. Actual motion generates lines and these lines seem to be less abstract than the points at their intersections, the intersections not being literal crossings existentially. There is no cosmic graphpaper or map; no place of places. The coordinates of human measurement are human instruments, not natural points. To call this space-time continuum a field is metaphorical; it is unlike an agricultural field or the electromagnetic field. It means nothing to say that it is static, or moving, or relative, or empty. The more primitive cosmologies call it "the wideopen spaces, the void." "What" it is may be a mystery. Suffice it to say that though it is itself not a map or calendar, it serves as orientation for all maps and calendars, all compasses and clocks, all distances and intervals, all places and dates. It defines beginnings and endings, but has itself neither beginning nor end. Some say it is everywhere at all times, others say it cannot be said to be at all. Its function as a universal frame for motions is all we can safely affirm of it.

INTERACTION IN THE ELECTROMAGNETIC FIELD

The home of nature's energies is called the electromagnetic

field, but how long it will continue to bear this name, with its medieval associations, seems uncertain in view of nuclear research. Here it is that radiations collide and power is generated. Whether it is also the field in which "forces" do their "acting," raises issues that need not concern a mere ontologist. Let us be content to call this the general realm of interactions, whatever the physics of these processes may turn out to be. We know already that the familiar radiations of heat, sound, light, and magnets are small segments of a world of waves. The ancient mythologies that pictured the ocean of being as ruffled by the transient waves of individual being may be revived as convenient models. This world of events occasionally eventuates in occasions, and occasions take on durable patterns and routes. Light rays concentrate in vision and other rays, in radios. All kinds of things and doings are generated in this power house. If nature has a center, this is it.

THE ENDURANCE OF CAREERS

There is a third field, which may be called natural history. It is, of course, not the field of written history, but the endurance of natural beings that have careers. Here it is important to distinguish two basic types of careers: the evolution, endurance, and perishing of inorganic individuals; and the life-spans of the living. In both cases there are beginnings, mid-careers, and endings. Certain humanist and existentialist philosophers are unwilling to concede careers to nonliving beings and a few of them even restrict careers to mankind. Thus Jean-Paul Sartre writes:

> Man is the only being by whom destruction can be accomplished. A geological plication, a storm do not destroy—or at least they do not destroy directly; they merely modify the distribution of masses of beings. There is no less after the storm than before. There is something else. Even this expression is improper, for to posit otherness there must be a witness who can retain the past in some manner and compare it to the present in the form of no longer. In the absence of this witness, there is being before as after the storm—that is all.[3]

To be sure, the destruction of a being and the creation of another are not the destruction or creation of matter. But to deny individuality and otherness to nature in the absence of human "witness" is not doing justice to natural history. Birth and death, too, "modify the distribution of masses," but to conclude that "masses of beings" have no individuality and no destructibility, that "being" remains after the storm as before and "that is all," is a very illiberal description of natural being, and an unjustified impoverishment of natural science.

Let us, then, in protest begin our analysis by paying due respect to the career of our solar system (even though the knowledge of that career seems more hypothetical than ever). Certainly we have sufficient evidence that stars grow cold, that nebulae are generated, that galaxies are changing, and in general that the heavenly bodies have histories, to force us to recognize definite processes and patterns among the stars. "Re-

3 Jean-Paul Sartre, *Being and Nothingness*, translated by Hazel E. Barnes (New York; Philosophical Library, 1956) p. 8.

distribution of masses" is not a sufficient description of these processes. Similarly, coming down to earth, the careers of lakes, valleys, mountains, gems (seen and unseen) are processes involving the creation and destruction of particular things, and natural history is composed of many such stories of many kinds of individuated "masses."

Man-made machines, too, have natural careers in addition to their non-natural creation. They naturally wear out, and are subject to the hazards of mechanical failures and accidents. It would be tedious to mention the various illustrations that might be collected, if it were necessary to prove the existence of finite careers among inanimate beings. Nature is full of beginnings and endings, of clashes and cataclysms, of ruined careers and contingencies. Existence is insecure and "aleatory" even without the dangers to life, and many a natural history reads like a tale of adventure. Of course, if terms like "career," "ruin," "accident," seem too loaded with human experience to be applied to inanimate things, to astronomical and geological processes, I shall not insist on them provided the facts of natural individuality and endurance be not obscured. A solar system is the classical model of a mechanical individual. In their natural functioning mechanical systems are not perfectly closed, not perfectly isolated and insulated; there is enough continuity in the dynamic field to absorb leakages of energy from many practically independent systems. Even the solar system leaks, and a bit of friction keeps any actual machine from being mechanically perfect. Hence a mechanism has individuality, endurance, misfortunes.

I cite Merleau-Ponty's definition of a physical system:

A physical system is a group of forces in a state of equilibrium or of constant change, such that no law can be formulated for its parts separately and that each vector be determined in magnitude and direction by all the others. Any local change will therefore produce a form, by a redistribution of the forces, which keeps their relation constant. It is this internal circulation of forces that *is* the system as a physical reality, and it is no more a composite of parts that are separable than a melody, which can always be transposed into other keys, is made up of the particular notes that give it momentary expression. A physical form which has such an internal unity inscribed in a segment of space and which is enabled by its circular causality to resist decomposition by external forces is an individual.[4]

This definition substitutes for Aristotle's unity of form and matter a functional unity of forces. But in either case, there is an admission that the "parts" are not as concrete or as individual as the whole.

Mechanical causation is a systematic correlation of energies and not mere "spontaneous variation." A machine can be identified and its functioning described as a particular process. The mechanism of the circulation of the blood in an organism can be identified and analyzed, whether the whole organism is a mechanism or not. A machine is known by what it does and by the ability of natural science to explain how it does it. There

---

[4] I translate from his *La Structure du Comportement* (Paris; Presses Universitaires, 1942) pp. 147-8.

are now many machines which are not natural in origin, but even manufactured machines function naturally, mechanically, and should be assigned their due place in nature. Man contributed much to natural mechanics, even before he added to the solar system. Mechanics is not a science of origins but of functionings, and therefore we must accept the mechanical products of man's inventiveness and art as existing in nature, and as existing in a way that is different from the existence of the manufacturer. A factory coordinates mechanical systems in addition to being an industry. A pipeorgan may be designed for the praise of God but it is also designed as a mechanism. Any mechanism, in short, works naturally, whether or not it be natural in origin and aim. The distinction between mechanical processes and the designing of machines should be clear enough. It is not necessary to assume that a mechanism is designed, or that it cannot be identified as an individual, except in terms of what it produces. A machine may or may not be productive. The solar system can be known adequately as a particular mechanical structure without raising any teleological questions. "To what end is nature?" asked Emerson, and almost any child might do the same. But it would be childish to think that the solar system cannot be understood before it is known how it contributes to the careers of galaxies, which careers in turn would have to be known as individual designs for specifiable ends. This is no way to try to understand nature, even though it may be the most elementary question in the case of machines made by man. It would be philosophically important, of course, if man could have a way of knowing what uses the solar system and the galaxies may serve. But lacking such knowledge, we must be content with the childish answer which Emerson gave to his childlike question, namely: nature exists to make natural science possible. Natural individuality is first of all mechanical integration, and though the science of mechanics is one, machines are many, whether celestial, cybernetic, or physiological.

Turning now to living beings, we are surely not using the term "career" figuratively when we apply it to their mode of being. Life-spans or lifetimes furnish the favorite and classic examples of temporal being. In the case of organisms, the processes of becoming, growth, health, disease, frustration, decline, death constitute careers which are clearly individualized—the natural stuff of stories. What the fact of organic life and structure adds to the theory of careers is not finitude, but tragedy and comedy, values and struggles.

FEELING AND VALUATION

Organisms are active, not merely interactive. They grope their way into the world and seek their proper livelihoods. They feel needs or, if they cannot feel, at least they exhibit needs. Where there are needs there are values, goods and evils, things to be appropriated or avoided. Organisms are selective and more or less competitive. They have their natural ways and skills, from the climbing of the vine to the arts of man. Their life is a composite of selection and effort. Such careers open up another dimension of natural being.

Success and failure are basic themes for such careers. By their natures or structures organisms are impelled or propelled, as the case may be, to engage in very specialized types of activity and to lead diversified careers. They act, as Aristotle, Heidegger, and Sartre have explained, as if there were privation in their being, something particular of which they are being deprived. They are not so much in pursuit of happiness, as engaged at a naturally ordained task of supplying the missing. What their particular values and disvalues are is usually to be determined not by their aim or final good, but by a critical observation of their more immediate needs, what they have accepted or appropriated, and what they have rejected. Few organisms look far ahead, and all but the most intelligent are absorbed in the demands of the present. Values are discovered opportunistically, not prospectively. This natural trait of organisms to be perpetually engaged in troublesome situations makes of them not beings dominated by an existentialist anxiety about they know not what, but beings dominated by a practical predicament of making the most of limited opportunities here and now. Plants are Epicureans, exploiting sunshine and rain day by day, and animals are more apt to be Stoics, willfully engaged in control, but both make a career by meeting concrete obstacles and opportunities as best they can. Nature provides engagements for all and success for the elect. This state of living nature is a state full of care (caution and discrimination are at a premium) and it is a struggle (since not all living possibilities can be realized), but it is not literally a struggle for existence, nor a struggle *for* anything, nor a war of all against all; it is ordinary trouble.

Such processes—let me say such behavior—make it necessary to distinguish a fourth field of nature, which I shall label "selectivity," for within it are found the processes which I have described as "natural selection," that is, active appropriation or rejection by natural beings.

Among the amazing properties of nature is the existence of actual possibilities or competing powers. This is quite distinct from pure or theoretical possibility as an imagined realm of being in an imaginary world. To derive possible worlds of *n* dimensions from the theory of "logical space" is a logical problem which need be no concern of ours in the ontology of nature. Actual possibilities are potential energies of a field for organic activities. In all chemical reactions, to be sure, there are specific sensitivities or material individualities of interaction. There is sensitivity in the plate of a camera which "responds" to the impact of light waves or X rays. But such discrimination in an optical apparatus is quite different from the sensibility of sense organs. Sensibility is the capacity to engage in feeling, and feeling is a process, not a field or film. When light is focussed on a living retina of a working eye it generates an activity of selection as well as a pattern of sensation. The camera does not generate action, whereas the retina operates a

switchboard for motor response. Both may be chemical processes, but they are very differently structured. In the living
eye the vision generates signals and the signals are transform-
ers. Mechanisms for groping, appropriating, and rejecting,
are ambiguity solvers; the actual possibilities are the ambigui-
ties in the field which call for selective activity. The so-called
"causal chain" is not an apt metaphor for this structure; a
"causal network" would be a better analogy. The feeling
organism drags its net through the field of powers, actualizing
some and leaving others potential. The point of using such a
model is to represent feeling not as "concretion" out of the
abstract, but as selection among powers.

Where there is life, there is nature; but there is also elementary valuation. Values are relative to feeling; the feeling
process transforms the field into positive and negative values
for an organism. This creation of values does not necessarily
imply conscious selection or awareness of values. The selective
process in organic vision and hearing and other forms of sensation is prior to the more developed processes of conscious selection and sense perception. Values are created before they are
known. Adam and Eve had their "eyes opened" to "the divine
knowledge of good and evil" by an act of eating. Tasting can
open one's eyes to values, but such acquaintance with good and
evil in the context of a life of toil is still far removed from
theoretical vision. Values come into being in the course of
nature, but they lead on to the arts of culture.

FINALITY, LEARNING, AND HABITS

Lastly we come to those processes of learning which lead out of the natural contexts into the fields of culture and to a very different type of orientation. The field of finality has been over-dignified as "the kingdom of ends." This noble kingdom is, by the better brands of ontologists, kept free of nature's domains. But, treading as I am in the paths of Woodbridge, I must ask you to take a careful, cautious look at natural teleology. Admitting with him that the human pursuit of happiness carries us beyond any natural orientation or earthly paradise, we must examine human nature and the behavior of other animals to discover whether the means-end relation has a natural home and origin.

I have intentionally described the process of feeling as it shows itself in natural beings in such a way as to free the analysis of living sensibilities from the postulate of animal faith in means toward ends. In its primary forms feeling is neither blind nor faithful; it is experimental without understanding the experiment as an operation. Selective action does not necessarily imply action in view of an end. The emotional life has a considerable range of frustrations and enjoyments, a considerable acquaintance with failure and success, with negative and positive values, before it learns the arts of prospective reference toward the ends of seeking. Value experience is more primitive than the discovery of utilities, for tasting good and evil precedes learning to know good and evil.

Learning and habit formation, which is intelligence's rooting in nature, begins with learning "the hard way," profiting by past pains in making a choice. But neither the recall of pains nor the acts of choice need be functions of awareness. The learning can be explained by conditioning; conditions are not final causes. A rat can learn the path to food without literally feeling hunger or knowing frustration as such. Innocent human beings too learn in much the same ratlike way; a subconscious retrospection leads to the formation of subconscious complexes. The so-called drives of human nature are not propellers but compulsions. It is possible, in fact quite common, for bodies to be intelligent without having any ideas. But among the brighter class of human beings there dawns somewhere along the path of learning the ability and then the habit to look ahead and to become aware of where the use of means is leading.

Such analysis is elementary psychology. The ontologist's problem is to observe such behavior in the context of the entire development of learning in order to perceive where and how the purposiveness of the process, which is evident to the ontologist as well as to the psychologist, passes from the domain of nature into that of culture. Both animal intelligence and conscious education are examples of finality. For the analyst, if not for the learner, all learning is structurally conditioned by the field of finality, the means-end relation. He should know better than the learner "what" is being learned. By examining "how" the learning is done he can determine whether the learner is a natural being or a cultural being or both.

Note: WOODBRIDGE AND DEWEY ON NATURE

I have distinguished the basic fields and processes in ways which cross the conventional distinctions between man and nature, for I have put man into nature, which is his original habitat. I have linked inorganic with organic "careers," whereas living processes are usually distinguished sharply from the inorganic. I have associated many aspects of human nature, including the primitive forms of learning, consciousness, and intelligence with those of other animals, and reserved only the more organized, systematic, and methodical developments of art and mind as cultural operations or experience. In general I have regarded relations of interaction as natural processes and those of transaction as cultural. But I am aware that it is useless to draw sharp lines here.

As a commentary on such problems, and especially on Woodbridge's views, I am appending a letter which John Dewey wrote to me July 15, 1949. It contains some significant reflections by Dewey on his own terminology and also suggests his opinion about Woodbridge's concept of nature.

In writing a new Introduction to *Experience and Nature* I wanted to convey two things: the first one was that while in the main and for "essence" I still stood by the discussions of the text, I now saw as I did not when I wrote that "experience" is a term or designation of what is specifically *human* as of a certain period—roughly speaking, the beginning with the rise of the new astronomy and physics in their opposition to the Greek and Medieval cosmological science— from now on I should prefer the word "culture." While, were I writing on the interpretation of the history of philosophy, I should make a point of culture being such at various important previous periods that other words stood for what was human in its connection with natural; this being a part of the view that the relation of the human to the natural has always been, under cover, the standing problem of philosophy, and its only justification for existence— science covering nature, so that philosophy must *use* science, but is absurd as a kind of science or rival to it. Roughly speaking, "the natural" is best seen as that which *isn't* human in its origins—physical and physiological, though these sciences are human in origin as well as in eventuation. With respect to *what* is taken as human and as natural there is a curious ambivalence on both sides.

I imagine that "interactivity" has to be construed in a somewhat different way from Newton's "equal and in opposite direction . . . reactions." I don't think the correction of the strictly mechanistic interpretation of this formula justifies "humanization" a la White-head, but is perhaps expressed in the new relativity that puts space into time so to speak—and thereby, speculatively speaking—makes possible the development of the physical into the physiological.

I fancy the Woodbridgean *Nature* as continuity of all contexts is a case of the ambivalence of "nature" in that nature is no longer supra-natural. But while I believe in the naturalness of man's arrival as an important aspect of their connection, I can't believe—or don't as yet —it does away with their distinction.

III. CULTURAL BEING

When René Descartes confessed that he, René, was doing some thinking, he called the world's attention to only one of a number of processes in which he was engaged, any one of which would have committed him to existence and some of which might be even less dubitable than his thinking and certainly less dubitable than his doubting. He was living, breathing, eating and drinking, resting from military service, tending the stove, and writing a book. If he had wished to call attention merely to his processes such as living, breathing, resting, or even the process of *cogitatio*, which often flows on irresponsibly, he might have used them perfectly well to prove his bodily, natural existence. He was evidently thinking of himself, his ego, his person, and he called attention to something that he, René, was doing. He proved his existence as an agent. Such activities as tending the stove, writing a book, or even merely writing his famous sentence are much better evidence than his breathing or sleeping.

Similarly I now shift your attention from the human animal to the human person and from natural processes to actions or operations. When we turn from processes to procedures we enter a new realm of being, which, in contrast to nature, is conveniently called culture.

Long before Homo sapiens was sapient he was at work. He gave up his easy life in nature's wild-apple orchard and began earning his living by working his brow. In this self-domesticating process, which did not begin with agriculture nor take place because of a sudden fall from innocence, the human animal gradually emerged, and still emerges, into the status of a worker whose operations are instrumental and experimental. Other animals, too, are busy and methodically busy, and it may be that in their early history they, too, learned the hard way the intricate habits which now instinctively shape their existence. And it may be that man, too, may degenerate into a wonderfully equipped instinctive busybody like the ants, bees, and birds, whose operations are not labor in the human sense, but sheer nature. But for the time being and for some time to come, mankind is a laboring animal in a unique sense, condemned, as the existentialists tell us, to the freedom of devising operations, and to taking the consequences for better or for worse. Adam and Eve got this idea, contrary to divine advice, and their children inherit this so-called original sin. It seems to be relatively original among animals; at any rate, no other animal has carried its labors to the "dignity" of man's.

It was assumed by T. H. Huxley and by other biologists in the heyday of romanticism that this human effort, which Huxley called the "horticultural process," was a defiance of nature and a struggle against natural selection. Today it seems to be less anti-natural and more supranatural. It is the ability to use natural resources as resources for human culture. Agriculture is the most obvious illustration, but all the stages in man's self-domestication bear witness to man's increasing ability to make nature operate for him and to invent mechanical slaves to facilitate his operations.

Because man has harnessed so many natural beings and processes to help him at his work and play (for we must use "work" here to embrace all man's productions and efforts), we have become accustomed to speak of the "operation" of natural forces. We say that the moon operates on the waters, that geological processes operate to form mountains and valleys, and that gravitation produces planetary systems. This is metaphor, and when we read "operations" into nature we speak anthropomorphically. When Newton analyzed natural motions into equal and opposite reactions of forces and calculated components precisely, he was preparing the way for the steam engine. After all, it was Newton and not nature that was geometrizing. And it is men and not bees that are in business. Perhaps the Scholastic Latin terms may serve to express this distinction between *natura naturata* and *opus operatum*, between a natural process completed and a human job done, between an eventuation and a production.

EXPERIENCE AND METHOD

I shall use the term "experience" as the process of learning by operating. This is the ancient, nontechnical use of *technē* to mean acquired skill or learned know-how. Recently "technology" has become popular among educators to designate empirical learning. Whatever the term used, it means long, methodical, intelligent work which eventuates in achievements, skills and products. To a worker who operates successfully in this way we shall give the honorable title of "a person."

The basic danger which threatens all persons as learners and which threatens human culture as a whole is the tendency to become prematurely learned. It is natural to rest from one's labors and on one's labors, and against this natural process workers must be constantly on guard. Professors are amused at the sophomore who, after a year's course in Contemporary Civilization, knows it all; and students are saddened by professors who, being learned, learn no more. Skills become habitual and operations become routine. Technicians do not engage in research and invention. When highly cultivated persons organize as an intelligentsia, real intelligence and culture are in danger. There is no end of work, for one achievement leads to another and no one knows where this procedure may carry mankind. But there are good reasons for fearing that operations may stagnate and that men may settle down into their cultivated routines and eventually become as automatic as the other animals. Forces beyond human control may put an end to the field of culture and the operations of experience. Man may learn no more and may join the other animals in the "state of nature" from which he has now departed. By its own nature the field of culture is infinite and by their own nature the operations of experience are endless, but there is nothing in the world to guarantee that existence will always have this cultural dimension, seeing that there was a time when the earth was without it. We are here in the midst of contingent being, and in our efforts to make the most of it, we may well make the worst of it.

PERSONALITY AND INDIVIDUALITY

A human infant begins its career as a natural organism or individual, making a mass of movements. But being born into a cultural matrix it gradually acquires personal traits. Its organic individuality is a prerequisite, but its personality is the outcome, not the presupposition, of its cultural being. Persons are made, not born; they are neither created nor uncreated. First, on its way to becoming a person, the child acquires a *"mind"* in the process of *"appropriating"* the operations of its particular cultural field. When it has a "mind of its own" it is able not merely to do its own work, but to understand what is implied in participation in a culture. It understands the works of others and their relations to its own work. It is this participation in the operations of a culture which gives to the growing individual his ontological status as a person among persons. For culture is an interpersonal relation and no individual can confer personality upon itself. A person is necessarily a social being.

The task of appropriating the operational complex of the

cultural matrix is the central problem of education, for education fails if it fails to produce a mind. There are pathetic souls, one hates to call them persons, who imagine that in order to be an integrated personality it is necessary to be homogenized culturally. This illusion is tragic as well as pathetic when it exists among educators. For individuals must do their own appropriating, and this is a difficult operation with which schooling too often interferes. It is rare that an individual finds himself born into a well-integrated culture. Diversity of interests, multiplicity of attractions and aversions, conflicts of groups and institutions, competing obligations and values—all these traits of a typical modern community must be not merely endured nor merely absorbed, but ordered into a set of attitudes, opinions, habits, decisions which transform an organic individual into a functioning person. A person "is" a mind which an individual acquires and owns as "his" mind. I am using "mind" here in perhaps too broad a sense, to signify the personality structure. To make out of the world as it is one's "own" world, or to transform a piece of the world into one's "own" environment is the primary task in the formation of a person, and it is a task for his mind primarily. When this is achieved the world has perspective, "his" perspective and he can recognize his point of view. This self-orientation in the cultural field is a distinctive focus and integration of interests.

Personality structure is being interpreted by certain analytical experts as essentially a mask, concealing the real self, which is closer to human nature than to a particular culture. This is

question-begging analysis from the point of view of the theory
of reality. Why is culture less real than nature, or personality
less real than spontaneity? The learned analyst, of course, is
tempted to exploit the Latin meaning of *persona* and to interpret all acting as artificial stage play. Granting that "the world
is a stage", including the natural world, and that a person plays
a role on it, why should this theatrical metaphor lead us to conclude that no one ought to play a role in the world? If the roles
were arbitrarily assigned by a producer, the point might be
well taken, but it would apply better to man's being cast into
his natural environment than to his participation in his cultural
environment. In nature man is a creature, but in culture he has
his share in playwriting and staging. His acting is not the
acting-out of a preformed plot, but the creation of a personal
role within a complex of roles that are in the process of composition. To interpret the composition as artificial and the actor
as a masquerader, implies that there is a more genuine play
going on behind the scenes. This is theological propaganda,
not factual analysis. Failing the demonstration that a human
being could be something more genuine than a personality,
we can disregard the rhetoric of our learned unmaskers, except
when they are dealing with certain types of persons whose
façade is a face-saving device.

THE DIMENSIONS OF CULTURAL BEING

   An analysis of the cultural aspects of the self or person must
take account of four elements which, though they are rooted

in human nature, develop only in a cultural context. Cooperatively they are the mind in operation and each has its own way of developing in the learning process. The progress of a person and of a culture depends on: the funding of memory, the vesting of interests, the organizing of ideas, and the vitality of the imagination.

The funding of memory is the relating of the past to the present in such a way that the person's interests, ideas, and imagination can have at hand capital, gleaned from experience, as resources for meeting new problems. This need implies a continual rearranging of historical data and personal experience. Tom, Dick, and Harry—each has his personal present and past times—his present or past minute, hour, year, and generation. Their families, communities, and countries have their different pasts and presents. Culturally, present and past are indefinable and any historian is "seeing in a glass darkly" when he guesses what of the past is to be retained for present uses. The funding of the culture's memory by a professional historian may be of little use to Tom and Dick, very important for Harry. And the family traditions are apt to be even less reliable. Each person must use his own intelligence in creating an orderly file from the past in view of his probable needs of reference. This is his mental working capital.

Second, his interests must be vested in relation to his institutions. There must be specialization for self-expression, division of labor for efficiency, integration in terms of the available institutions through which the interests can be developed, selection to avoid distraction, and variety to avoid boredom. Instrumental labors and intrinsically enjoyable activities must be balanced; luxuries balanced against needs. In a typical modern community the opportunities for gratifying interests are sufficiently extensive to embarrass a person engaged in the problem of organizing and investing his own interests prudently. Civilization is built on discontents; but when the discontents instead of the interests become vested a culture is doomed.

Third, the interests must generate ideas, and new ideas must regenerate old interests. An interest cannot be vested if it fails to be conceptualized. Symbolization and communication are among the most basic tools of self-expression and self-understanding. Through them an interest is generalized and transpersonalized; the sharing of interests becomes normal. Ideas, as they enter into operation, work a marvelous transformation and become a distinctive kind of being. Ideas take on the form of work-ahead, jobs, tasks, problems, plans, methods, enterprises. These concepts, to use the rhetoric of Etienne Souriau, hover over the interests of a worker like guardian angels or guiding spirits.[1] The Greeks, as usual, had a good word for them; they called them hypotheses—things put-over or put-under. These are the stuff all experiments and some lectures are made of. They come and go in mysterious, unexpected ways and with incalculable power.

Lastly, interests and their ideas must be nourished by

1 cf. Etienne Souriau, "La mode de l'existence de l'oeuvre-à-faire," *Bulletin de la Société française de Philosophie* (1956).

imagination. Imagination at work accompanies ideas at work. Without each other neither is effective. The kind of imagination I am calling to your attention is not inborn, is not the imagination discussed in works on human nature; it is a cultural, creative, personal achievement. How it is achieved, I do not know; but everyone knows persons, voluble persons, who are without it. I have read many books and articles on this subject, but most of them were too unimaginative to be informative.

Recently a very young student showed me the design of a new kind of computer he was inventing. On its top the machine had a head-like glass bulb which flashed whenever it got an idea. It was ironic to see how unaware the child was that it was describing its own head; its eyes were flashing as it described the design. A computer which would be imaginative and not merely an information giver, would be a great help indeed, for ideas still come at too long intervals to human heads.

It is difficult to avoid the metaphors of illumination when speaking of imaginative ideas. "Insight," "inner light," "light of nature," these are conventional substitutes which explain nothing. The language of "inspiration" or mental vitality is a bit closer to the facts, for an inspired body "gets going." Imagination is a form of energy and not a dreaming. I cannot say precisely what it is, though it is the very essence of a lively mind. If it is a light, it is not "the light of nature" but rather of culture. It saves methodical ideas from stagnation and keeps

procedures progressing. I need say no more on this subject since
Justus Buchler has explored it thoroughly in connection with
his work on method.[2]

I have indulged in the commonplaces of the psychology of
experience because I need to refer to it as background for the
chief topic of analysis, namely, the categorial dimensions of
cultural being. By dimensions of culture I mean those basic
structures or fields within which cultures take on their varied
patterns and achieve their varied works. There are four that
appear to be basic, irreducible, categorial:

A. Historical being—the funding of experience.

B. Moral being—the field of institutional transaction.

C. Coexistence—the methodical development of interests.

D. Communion—imaginative personal relations.

HISTORICAL BEING

History, of course, deals with events and all events are in
nature. Consequently historical being, though it is cultural, is
related to and part of the general course of events and their
causes and consequences in the natural order of causation.
Natural happenings continually intrude on the course of
human operations (which are the immediate subject of history)
and learning the significance of such happenings is a part of
man's historical experience. But admitting this we do not admit that human history is a chapter in natural history or

2 Justus Buchler, *The Concept of Method* (New York; Columbia University
Press, 1961).

evolution and that historical explanation is the same as physical explanation. Scientific historians have been tempted from time to time to construct a physics of history and to use this construction to predict the necessary sequence of human affairs. These attempts at purely naturalistic history have proved to be fantastic and also disastrous. Consequently historians have become cautious in their attempts to be scientific on a model of physical science, and have developed their own methods of telling historical truth as accurately and as objectively as possible.

But our concern is not with the science of writing history but with the subject matter of historical science. What does it mean to be an historical being? The most common assumption is that since persons have careers, their history must also be a career. Whether we know its beginning and end or not, it must have a beginning or "dawn" and come to a close. Working on this assumption, historians try to locate the probable middle of history or to plot the "rise and fall," or the evolution of man, on a biological model. History then is a simple story and can be understood as a whole.

The futility of this attempt to conceive historical being as a single career is now generally admitted. But the reason why this is not a true account of historical being is not our ignorance of beginning and end, but a better knowledge of what the past is. History deals with an actual past and not with a segment of the natural course of events in natural time.

Historical being is complicated by the fact that historical

time is unlike natural time. History is divided into past, present, and future *times;* there is no such temporal structure in
nature. The past and future are relative to a present and the
present is real in human experience, though in clock time past
and future practically meet except for a theoretical "momentary" present or instant of time.

Our analysis of historical being must therefore begin with
an analysis of what "being present" means. I quote a typical
attempt to explain the present:

> The present is not capable of becoming the material of thought.
> While we think in the present, *what* we think of is either past or
> future. . . . And yet without a present we could neither have a future
> or a past. Although it is not capable of being presented in thought, it
> is that which makes past and future possible conceptions of thought.
> The present is that in which we live and think, that which we must
> have, and that which we want to have. . . . What we want is the
> present, even though to adjust it to our liking we need thought with
> its conception of a future. And it must not be overlooked that the
> present is that which makes all else possible.[3]

From the point of view of human experience and culture it
is the present time that we have with us always. It is most
actual. Its past has been and its future will be; only the present
is in operation. The present, however, is merely a collective
name for the present times of all those persons who are in
operation and for whom their present is actual time for work
and play and thought. History, then, has this moving, un-

---

3 Stephen Ward, *The Ways of Life* (Oxford; Oxford Univ. Press, no date
[written about 1914]), pp. 66-67.

stable center—the eternal now of actual time. There is nothing "specious" about this present, though its boundaries are indefinite. It is a thoroughly real duration.

However, it is dependent on having a past (not on having had a past). It must carry its historical past with it into the future, and this "living" past in the present is that portion of what has been which it has funded for reference and recall when needed. Hence historical composition must be up-to-date, continually shaping its perspectives to a changing present. Of all the sciences, historical science is most in danger of the disease which John Wriston has aptly named "hardening of the categories." There is in the historian's profession a delicate equilibrium between invention and discovery, selection and accuracy, generalization and truth. In short, all of us, even more than the trained historians, are treading here on shifting sands of time, and need a bigger and better past as our present expands. Or, on the contrary, as a French existentialist warns us, we are being robbed of our future because so much of our past is meaningless for our narrow present. Enduring a relatively isolated present and an historical disorientation may call for an appeal to the "courage to be," but more needful than encouragement is a thorough reorientation and demythologizing of our historical being. And this is a task for historical intelligence rather than for present courage. It is not our present that is to blame, but the speciousness of our historical imagination.

Building, maintaining, and using one's past—intelligently

funding human experience—is an operation in which imagination as well as memory plays an important role. This is even
more evident in the anticipation of the future. Prediction depends largely on reflection. It is impossible to possess a future
in any significant, mental sense without possessing a mature
past. Consciousness, being aware or having a full present is
precisely the interplay of past and future, the bringing together
of the learned and the to-be-lived. What Montague used to
call pure "sciousness" without the "con," would be sheer
emotion without meaning. "Having a mind" and "being historical" are therefore two ways of describing the same fact of
experience. It is seldom that the changes in one's present life
are precisely the events anticipated, for even the most carefully
funded past is only an approximate guide to the future. If the
future were known as well as the past, mental life would be an
intolerable bore and would eventually cease entirely. It is the
guessing one does as one looks into the future that gives mental being its inherent direction and gives empirical time its
flow. What is ahead of us is what our heads are full of, and without this imagination of what is to be, the so-called becoming
present of the future would have no excitement in it. The dis-
parity between what comes to be and what was supposed to
become is what keeps the mind alive and incites interests. This
gamble in historical existence, which is known among metaphysicians by the more dignified name of contingency, is the
essence of the present and its meanings, the union of what the
German ontologists call *Dasein* and *Sosein*.

MORAL BEING

A second categorial dimension of cultural being is the realm of obligation. Though moral being, like historical being or any other form of dynamic being, has its roots in natural processes, its specific structure is interpersonal and transactional. Man is a gregarious animal and finds natural contentment in group life. The classical idea of *homo homini lupus* (or of the war of all against all) is a mythical construction and owes whatever application it may have to human culture not to human nature. For men, like wolves, live in packs, and when they hunt do not prey naturally on their kind. Group life would no doubt be found in the human "state of nature," if such a state could be found among men. The belief in primitive or natural individualism and anarchy is unsubstantiated, and it is a contemporary curiosity that Jean Paul Sartre should have revived it. He pictures man as naturally, today as always, a solitary being living in a state of *collectivité* or mass juxtaposition without any genuine bonds or grouping. Being a dramatist, Sartre, no doubt like Hobbes, pictures this fantastic state of nature in order to give revolutionary glamor to the social "oath" or contract and to the "state of fusion" which characterizes civil society and moral obligation, or "engagement."

Man is naturally sensitive to the claims and needs of others, has some respect for himself and his fellows, and indulges in antipathies and indifferences to some while being attracted to others. Out of such sensitivities there grows, with the emergence of personality, an awareness of obligations and a recognition of the demands made by social situations. Empirically, obligations come prior to any general sense of duty or moral sense. The varied interests of intersecting groups create conflicting demands and out of these conflicts there emerge standards for membership in particular societies or associations, and there also emerge general norms for transactions, which deal with such conflicts, and a general sense of duty. A typical obligation is not a bare demand or categorical imperative but is accompanied by some recognition of reciprocity or some kind of "covenant." A transaction accompanied by such sanctions as are stated in the Ten Commandments of Deuteronomy: "for the enlargement of thy borders" or "that thy days may be prolonged and that it may go well with thee." As experience with obligations grows, the awareness of reciprocity as an essential condition of transactional relations grows, and a network of rights and duties is recognized publicly as a basic context of cultural being.

"Conscience makes cowards of us all." The general habit of refraining from impulses to violence, of respecting claims, and of keeping peace may appear to be a kind of animal cowardice, but it is also a basic form of cultural courage and cooperation.

Codes of law are usually preoccupied with means of enforcement and definition of sanctions for definite violations, but judgments of a court usually contain *obiter dicta* in which the pragmatic legal structure is rationalized. A classical example of such rationalization is contained in Justinian's basic code of Roman Law. He declared, "All men are born free and equal." As a matter of ordinary experience in matters of freedom and equality no proposition could be more evidently false. For no human being is born into a merely natural environment, men are born into society. And yet this dictum has come down through the centuries performing a useful function in moral theory. For in its legal context, the meaning Justinian intended to give was: no obligation and no social status is of natural origin; obligations and privileges accrue through institutional experience. But the more mythical and imaginative formulation has served to clothe the empirical observation about jural relations in the garb of a law of nature, to which men still appeal when their obligations become oppressive and their inequalities unjust. It serves to establish faith in natural law, whereas it was intended to magnify the role of human institutions. To sum up:

1) The field of obligation is limited to the field of interpersonal relations.

2) The field of obligation is not dependent on a conceptual order or system of general norms; it rests primarily on the reciprocal claims made upon each other when members of a community or a common interest engage in transaction.

3) The primary function of morality is not the definition of the good or of values, but the specification of the conditions required for cooperation.

4) Moral ideas are regulatory ideas in the sense of defining the general conditions of cooperation. They are not rules for the promotion of common values, but rules for the social conditions under which any value can be pursued. They regulate structure of transaction regardless of the particular values or ends in view.

5) Obligations are social, institutional beings whose reality is independent of the willingness of any person to recognize them. Conscience is not the *cause* of morals, but the *fruit* of moral experience.

Thus morality is a categorial dimension of cultural structure, irreducible to interests, ideas, arts, or sciences. It is a context or matrix within which these other aspects of cultural being function. The institutions of morality are as varied as vested interests and organized communities happen to be. Any organized group develops a moral structure which is by its nature the public frame of that group. Political societies or states create the most explicit and impressive moral structures, but they are not the only moral publics: churches, families, industries, labor unions, sports, generate relatively autonomous fields of obligation and forms of transaction.

COEXISTENCE

Having examined the funding of experience in history, and the framework of transaction in morals, we come now to the vesting of cooperative production in institutions—the arts of work and play, crude and fine, practical and theoretical, scientific and otherwise. In the arts and sciences mankind has preserved and systematized what it has learned to do, to think, and to cherish.

This cultural heritage has become so essential to man that he is inclined as he grows older to venerate it and ascribe to it the kind of inviolability which sacred beings possess. But a wise person, one who is truly experienced, takes his heritage for better or for worse. He must live *with* it and to a large extent *by* it, but he must also continually evaluate it. For values, as we have explained before, are the values of the living, and a heritage must prove its worth to each new generation. An eternally enshrined value, such as superstitious persons believe in, has lost its power in existence as an aspect of cultural being. Goods must be actively appropriated to be really good, and evils actively avoided to be really evil. To appropriate the whole heritage at once as an undigested mass of value, which seems to be what the traditionalists expect of us, is impossible physically and absurd morally. Institutions are the proper subject matter of criticism, and though they all come to us with the normative credentials of a teacher, their norms always are subject to validation. This does not imply that values and norms are transcendental to culture; it means that within any culture the living must learn how to regard the dead and what to do with the knowledge and skill offered to them by their inherited institutions. For, to repeat my primary point of ontology, these elements of culture are inherited as instruments for learning, not as resources of human nature.

As ontologists, then, we have the task of examining the arts and sciences in cultural operation, that is, as the forms of man's work. They have transformed labor by creating corporate beings, whose cooperation has given to human existence the dignity which often erroneously is attributed to human nature.

The most obvious trait of institutions is their proliferation—always more and more varied. The unity of the arts and sciences is conspicuously absent. Their values and their methods, their structures and their aims, even within the limits of a single community, are diversified, so that even if there is a political or moral solidarity, this unity is still far from creating a totalitarian structure of interests. What unity there is is to be found in the integration of interests in each personality. Such personal integration implies a choice among the abundance of vested interests, and therein lies the most real freedom. There are persons, usually authors of philosophies of culture, who sigh amid the contemporary confusion of interests for the integration of the Periclean or Augustan Ages, or the unity of Christendom, or primitive New England, or the ante bellum South, but these lovers of integrated cultures are usually dismayed when less nostalgic historians puncture their illusions about the past, and they would be even more disillusioned if they had to exist in closed society. Integration is a personal opportunity. The unity of arts or sciences is not worth seeking. The variety is more exciting and instructive. New media, many methods, varied tastes—these must now be taken for granted as essential to the being and well-being of any community.

A polarity of interests is exhibited by most cultures: the rhythm of work and play, labor and leisure. As play, too, becomes institutionalized and professionalized, this rhythm is somewhat obscured and corrupted. Increasingly the folk arts are being industrialized and professionalized. Stage plays, dancing, sports, and vacations are hard work for the players and passive entertainment for the spectators. Play is more than rest from work and recreation at its most authentic level is creative, productive. The idea that work is production and play is consumption is a symptom of decadence in ideas, in work, and in play. Almost any activity can become laborious and almost any labor can be recreational. A decent alternation enhances both work and play; the compensatory rhythm is more reasonable and human than so extreme a division of labor that some are mere slaves and others mere players.

An adequate theory of human operations and interests ought not dismiss the realms of arts and sports as mere superstructure, more or less parasitical, wastefully spending the earnings of genuine production. To produce a song or to play the piano is just as authentic a pursuit of human interests and needs as to raise vegetables, and some say that playing the horse races, too, is among the liberal arts. In such matters an ontologist has no criteria for judgment.

COMMUNION

For this last categorial dimension of culture I can find no adequate word; I wish to dissociate some things that are usually associated and to present as basically united some things that are usually dissociated. What remains to be described in the realm of culture is the most intimately personal and interpersonal dimension, the interest which persons have for each other as persons not as cooperators, as pals not as partners, as comrades not as fellow citizens. In some of the philosophical idioms, this is known as "intersubjective being." When subjects of interest get together, not in pursuit of objects of interest but in the enjoyment of each other as persons, they somehow avoid being objects to each other. They learn to share the processes of experiencing, not so much as operations designed to serve interests but as themselves mutually interesting.

The most obvious form of this cultural relationship, which I am designating by "personal communion," is friendship. Friendship is not an operation. It is not obligatory but spontaneous; however, it is not natural attraction but cultivated association. The classic analysis of friendship remains Aristotle's chapters on it which are central to his *Ethics* and *Politics*. Friendship is the essence of human well-being. In his analysis of civil existence (*politeia*) the categories of *koinonia* and *philia* are primary. Such an identification of neighborliness and friendship, of community and communion, is no longer possible in modern cultural analysis. There are still instances of such a personal unity in community, but they are the exception, not the norm.

Friendship is neither a union of bodies nor a meeting of minds. It is a form of society, not of union. Friends treat each other respectfully but not at a respectable distance. They share a common self-respect, if such language is permissible because it seems to be accurate. An essential qualification for friendship is having other interests besides friendship, for, like any other virtue, friendship in isolation becomes boredom. It takes a modicum of interesting experience and maturity to qualify one for friendship. Persons who imagine that they can be subjectively interesting without being objectively interested soon discover their miscalculation. Friendship is intensely imaginative without being primarily conceptual; it is emotional without being an obsession. Friends possess each other, but neither is the property of the other. Friendship needs cultivation, but it cannot be pursued as an art or a virtue. It appears to be a natural growth because it is unconsciously cultural. A genuine friendship, therefore, is recognized by the absence of formalities, pretence, stances and façades, and by the presence of communion.

A second form of communion is piety. By this term I mean devotion rather than devoutness. Devotion among persons? No, for that would amount to friendship. Devotion to one's work? No, for that would be merely intensified interest. Piety may not have a well defined object, but it shows itself whenever what is cherished is endangered. Many goods are accepted habitually without question and with only an occasional gesture of thanksgiving. There are other goods that are treasured because their possession is insecure. Devotion shows itself in defense. It is common in these warlike times to speak of "exis-

tential commitment." In the context of drastic conflicts such a
concept is intelligible enough, for one is often unaware of the
real objects of one's devotion until one discovers what one will
fight for.

George Santayana, in his exposition of Greek or "natural"
piety spoke of it as "loyalty to the sources of one's being." He
was probably reacting against the rhetorical formula of his col-
league, Josiah Royce, "loyalty to loyalty." Jonathan Edwards
had an idea of piety similar to Santayana's; he cultivated what
he called a "general consent to Being." In Edwards' followers
this virtue became somewhat histrionic, and devoutness is now
generally reproached. Without wishing to repudiate a sincere
"consent to Being", I wish to include in the concept of piety
some of the traits which Santayana reserved for what he termed
"spirituality", devotion to one's ends. Whether it be ideal
ends or natural resources that are cherished, it becomes appropriate in times of decision to try to confess consciously those
aspects of life and heritage to which one clings, and which at
times make demands on one's loyalty. A pious person is usually
embarrassed when asked to itemize the objects of his devotion.
It may be unreasonable to ask him to do so. Piety may well be
diffusive but it need not be either effusive or sentimental. The
poetic arts have also sought for worthy expressions and general
symbols for piety, but precisely because it is very personal the
attempts to create standardized, conventional, institutional
symbols and rites are seldom very successful. The religious arts
are among the most adequate expressions, but when they be-

come a routine or a duty they are apt to replace authentic devotion by ceremonial devoutness. Piety, like friendship, cannot be commanded.

I come lastly to speak of communion with spirits, which is the most imaginative and powerful aspect of communion. By spirits I mean ghosts, invisible, haunting persons. Some spirits are those of once living persons, who now have a vicarious being in the lives of others. Some spirits are purely imaginary beings who nevertheless have a personal power and real being in many generations of men.

In one of his sermons to his fellow-monks, Meister Eckhardt tries to make concrete and plausible the doctrine that "Being is more than life." His first illustration is the martyr, whose being begins with his death. This is a simple case of a well-known fact that many persons have post-mortem careers in the lives of others. They become parties to an intimate personal communion with the living. Besides the dead who "dare stir abroad" (Hamlet I: 1), there are fictitious spirits like Hamlet who never lived but who have this haunting power among the living. They are presented in biography, poetry, myth, icons, symbolical forms of many kinds, and are concrete and vivid enough to be genuine personalities though deprived of life.

In all cultures spirits are highly important powers, because the imaginative communion which they arouse among the living creates strong emotional and ideal bonds not only in individual persons but in societies and institutions. Such imaginative friendships and fellowships, to say nothing of terrors, add another dimension to personal existence.

First let us consider evil spirits, "familiar" communion with whom may lead to obsessions, to being possessed. Hitler still exercises a terrible power in many lives, and such power cannot be dismissed as fictitious or superstitious. Nor can it be called impersonal. I have met persons recently who at the very mention of F. D. R. shudder, and who cannot let the deceased rest but must continually brood over their ruin as being the personal work of a wicked genius.

Next, there are ancestral spirits to whom devotion continues to be paid in their homes. Anyone who has seen the memorial tablets on the domestic "spirit shelf" of a Chinese or Japanese home and who witnesses the rites connected with them knows that there is a "real presence" of past generations in the life of the family.

Then there are sainted spirits of holy men and women whose cultus makes them personally prominent in the lives of their devotees: St. Francis of Assisi, Mahatma Gandhi in India are well-known examples.

Lastly, there are "characters" of fiction that endure as personalities in the lives and imaginations of many generations. Whether Dr. Faustus lived or not makes little difference: Faust is a familiar type personified. So also Socrates (and not Plato!). Ulysses, Don Quixote, and Mickey Mouse make a curious trio—all three are present, have countless friends, and are now more personal than their authors.

The spirit world is well populated and diversified and powerful. My aim in presenting a few spirits at random is to show the difference between having communion with a spirit and having an idea. Spirits are symbolized in the mind and appear to the imagination but they are not conceptual beings; they are real, nonliving persons, entering as persons into the lives of others. Their being is more than mental and imaginary, for their power takes many forms: they are loved or feared; they form societies, influence economies, and affect governments; they stimulate art, philosophy, and religion. It is more appropriate to ascribe such deeds to the spirits themselves than to the books, statues, images, stories, authors through whom they have come into cultural being.

Communication with spirits has been attempted in many ways and has yielded more "encounters" than communication. But communion does not require conversation. Neither is it a one-way transaction or meditation. The communion may take no verbal form at all and yet involve an empirical, personal encounter. For while the living person is reading or seeing or hearing the story of what the spirit says or does, the spirit is taking hold of him as being present personally, though not physically; and the living may make an appropriate response, though the spirit is immovable.

The communion is by no means unrelated to the career of the spirit. Many a saint has become greater and greater because of the kind of communion generated by him. The growth of St. Francis in stature and power is a good illustration. Other spirits may have an opposite fortune and rapidly sink into oblivion. A spirit is not everlasting, for all persons are temporal constructs; but its being is not dependent on the life of its body; it has cultural determinants. The most unexpected and curious things can happen to spirits.

I cite only one example. The German poet Rainer Maria Rilke wrote a series of letters to a young struggling poet, and in a Christmas letter he offered to the discouraged poet the following Christmas message:

Why do you not think of him as He-who-is-to-come, who is everlastingly ahead, living in the future, the final fruit of the tree on which we are leaves? What prevents you from casting his birth into times to come, and why can you not live your life as though it were a painful, beautiful day in the course of a great pregnancy? Can't you see how all that happens is always another beginning? And might this not be *His* beginning, seeing that beginning is in itself something lovely? If he comes as the all-fulfiller, must He not be preceded by lesser beings, in order that He may have a fullness and surplus from which to choose? Must he not come last, that he may encompass all, and what meaning can our being have, if he for whom we are longing has already been?

Like bees gathering honey, so we take from all things their sweetest essences and construct Him. We begin our work with the small and even the unpromising tasks, if only we do them lovingly, and then we rest in silence or with a little lonely joy. And in all we do, alone without helpers and followers, we are making a beginning of Him whom to know in our life-time is no more possible than for our ancestors to know us. And yet they who have long been gone are in us, our concern, a burden of our destiny, our throbbing blood, and our character as it takes shape out of time's deeps.

Is there anything that can rob you of such a hope, to be some day in Him who is farthest on the frontier? Celebrate Christmas, my dear friend, in this pious attitude.[5]

To Rilke this mixture of Jesus, Nietzsche, and Zarathustra and of existentialist ontology was a genuine Christmas communion with the Holy Child, which was to him not a mere symbol or poetic fancy, but a loving companion of the dawn and the frontier, with whom he could have pious communion, here and now, though he looked for "His coming" in the future. To the recipient of the letter it was merely a mythological rendering of Rilke's philosophy.

It is common to refer to the being of spirits as a "spiritual life" or an "after-life" and to attribute a kind of life to them because they live vicariously in others. This is misleading rhetoric. But to insist that the dead may be cultural agents and have power is not a rhetorical ontology, though it may be misinterpreted. There is a big difference between being dead and not being. "To have been" does not imply, of course, "to be." But "to have been alive" does not mean that the person ceases when the body dies. It may be true to say that a person no longer living may join the company of spirits that never had bodies. But it may be that there is a significant difference between an historical person and a fictitious character. The one carries with him into history a real past life, whereas the other is a product of the imagination. However, in the long run the actual life may be negligible compared with the spiritual career

5 Translated from Rainer Maria Rilke, *Briefe an einen Jungen Dichter*: Letter from Rome, Dec. 23, 1903 (Wiesbaden; Insel Verlag, 1958) pp. 32-3.

in culture. There are many controversies about the "historical Socrates" and the "historical Jesus." The terms are ambiguous. A martyr death implies the death of a living body in the service of a cause. A martyr must have lived an heroic life which gave the noteworthy meaning to the death. But the powers of Socrates and Jesus throughout centuries of human experience are impressive careers of these persons and historically more conspicuous than their bodily lives.

On the other hand, to attribute immortality to spirits because some persons have careers that transcend their lives is also false. For the same reason that a person becomes actual by a process of experience following physical birth, a personality may be destroyed physically (as in the case of Nietzsche) long before its bodily death, and then exist as a spirit, or it may cease to have any influence apart from its body and die with the body, or it may linger disembodied among the living. A person that has a living body has life and he ceases to live when disembodied (or before, if the body ceases to support the person). A spirit does not have life, though it is a person, and therefore when its career among the living comes to an end, the end is only metaphorically a death. But this is a very different ontology from the Platonic doctrine of the immortality of the soul or the Christian doctrine of the resurrection of the body. There is a sense in which a spirit may be called a resurrected person, but when a person has not been buried the resurrection is really a transformation in being rather than a coming back into life.

Persons, whether alive or spirits, are individualities or personalities, patterns of life, characters, and must be distinguished from merely symbolical beings, like the muses and the unicorns, and from ideas, like the "spirit of truth" or "sheer beauty." Their careers as persons and personal powers are very different types of being from the careers of institutions, ideals, or galaxies. St. Francis is an idealized Francis of Assisi but he is no mere icon; he remains a person. Similarly there is a great difference between Santa Sophia (the Holy Wisdom) and the Blessed Virgin. There was a tendency in the early church to make "the Mother of God" iconic, like "the Father in Heaven," but popular piety and Renaissance art put an end to this tendency.

I may be expected to say something about "spirituality." I have avoided the term because it is ontologically useless, and in addition is being abused to such an extent that it seems to me the less said here about it the better.

A word of explanation is due, perhaps, about the Christian faith in the Holy Spirit or Holy Ghost. This is an entirely different use of the term "spirit." This Spirit of Truth was conceived as a divine breath (*pneuma*) and not a person in the sense that Jesus is a human personality. "Ghost" is a plain mistranslation, and the three "persons" of the Holy Trinity are three hypostases or revelations of the Divine Being. Of the three only Jesus is a person in the sense in which we are using the term. And communion with Jesus is an entirely different kind of worship from either belief in the Creator or faith in the coming to earth of the Holy Spirit of Truth.

IV. FORMAL BEING

ACTUALITY AND FORMALITY

Recently I had to speak in a small lecture room which had a fireplace. As I stood facing the audience I was increasingly haunted by the awareness that over the fireplace behind me there was a quotation from Emerson: "Life is our Dictionary." How many lectures seem to be based on this motto! And how different such lectures are from Emerson's essays. I can imagine a fellow-Yankee retorting to Emerson, "But often in life a real dictionary comes in mighty handy." Apparently Emerson was thinking, when he wrote this dubious epigram, about Noah Webster or some other real author of a dictionary who was continually obliged to refer from the dictionaries of others to life itself and life's usages. But a person who is faced with the problem of translating life into language, which is the basic problem of communication, knows very well that a dictionary is a very different kind of being from the users of a dictionary; it is useful to them precisely because it is formal and lifeless.

I pass now from the realm of actuality and its movements, activities, and experiences, to the realm of dictionaries, filing cabinets, computers, and formularies. This realm of systems is rapidly becoming so rich, manifold, infinite, that human beings are increasingly dependent for their existence on these inhuman, unnatural beings. We must examine the interplay between activities, on the one hand, and forms, symbols, systems, structures, on the other.

Formulation is, of course, a process and has its place in the realms of processes and of operations. But if we study what forms are independently of the process of formulation, we have before us a static way of being which is categorically unlike active being. It is not a single system or world order. The realm of orders is a profuse and fertile field within which many kinds of relations have their being, more compatible than coherent, not engaging in the struggle for existence. There is room for all and there seems to be a kind of infinite opportunity which allows systems to display their individualities, variety, independence. It would be an exaggeration to call this realm of orders a chaos. The theory of order is already confident that it could bring order out of any given chaos. But, and this is a very important but, a concrete chaos must be given to the formulator before he or it can get to work. There must be a program for formulation and not a mere theoretical, univeral chaos. Therefore an analytical ontology would do well to refrain from saying much about the order of orders or the structure of the world of all possible formulations. There are those who imagine universal order to be the best of all possible worlds, but, being a world of endless dictionaries, it is obviously no place to live.

It is customary to describe this world of forms as the realm of theory, mind, discourse, intelligibility, the noumenal world. If there were no living minds and no actual languages, this world would not be known, but the same trite observation would apply also to nature and culture. To observe this world "in itself," per se, independent of the world of experience, is therefore an impossibility. But it is possible for us, as minds engaged in ontological knowledge, to dismiss temporarily the process and problem of experiencing this world and to study what is known of it as something real, not as if it were nothing but a human utility. Keeping in mind that there is an actual world by which this nonactual world is discovered to be, we can abstract what has been discovered to be and how it happens to be from the minds that make this discovery. Having engaged in this work of abstraction we can then turn about and face the world of actuality from which we came and try to understand how we can travel in and out of the world in which we live in order to acquaint ourselves with the internal relations among the propositions, ideas, theories, orders, proportions which we use in life, but whose way of being is not ours.

I shall not attempt to make a systematic exposition of this realm of formality, partly because I am incompetent to do so, partly because such a task would be too exhausting to be practical, even if it were theoretically possible. Suffice it to describe a few basic types of formal systems. My primary task here is to exhibit a sufficient variety of structures to prove that this realm is not confined to conceptual or theoretical systems and cannot properly be restricted to the world of discourse, logic, or mind. However, I shall begin with the things of the mind.

REASON

Among thinking beings a proposition is a proposal or a judgment, an hypothesis or a decision, put in communicable form. Communication is an operation and transaction among minds. The things transacted, transmitted or translated are commonly called ideas or concepts. The term "idea," like the term "theory," is derived from the process of vision. The mind is said to have an "inner eye" and to "behold" not only ideas but the order among ideas. This visual terminology is metaphorical, but the metaphor is so pervasive and persistent that it is very difficult to express operations of conceiving without falling into the language of perceiving. "I see" or "Don't you see?", used in the context of argument, are our most common expressions for "understanding." "I understand" is a less concrete diction than "I see," but it is at least less metaphorical, since no one understands what "to understand" means literally. "Conceiving" at least suggests a social act, like "communication" or "agreement." Perhaps the best usage is the colloquial, "Do you get it?", which suggests a mental grasping or "mentipulation." Whatever the physics and psychology of "ideas" may be, let us agree to call a group of ideas, systematically related to each other, abstracted from the empirical situations of communication in which they function, a "rational order." In other words, let us take the "cons," "pros," "pers," from "ceptions" and "spections" and let us look at the formal relations which bind ideas to each other.

The first notable trait about the being of ideas is that they cannot exist singly; they are by their nature systematic and interrelated. The same proposition may be expressed in many languages; the languages are somewhat correlated and make translation possible. However, most important is the fact that any language has a systematic character, so that ideas in any language belong to a system of linguistic or syntactic structure. In addition, propositions imply each other or contradict each other. No idea, therefore, can exist per se; it is by its very structure part of a network of logical relations quite apart from its entanglement in discourse. The relations that govern coherence of meaning assign to any proposition its proper place in a logical structure. This structure is commonly called the rational order or the realm of reason. Coherent sequences of propositions segregate those that belong and those that do not belong together. There are then at least four basic contexts in which any idea exists; its two actual relationships to nature and to culture, and its two formal systems of symbolism and of implication.

FACTICITY AND TRUTH

Some ideas belong to a fifth order. If they make assertions about matters of fact, they enter into a system of evidence or knowledge of nonformal beings. These systems constitute the sciences as bodies of verified statements about events, processes,

bodies, careers, histories, cultures, in the actual world. These
bodies of factual knowledge, which we shall call collectively
"truth," are not unrelated to reason. They too are rational structures more or less, never entirely. A rational structure functioning in a cognitive structure is called an explanation. The sciences
are attempts to give systematic form to varied kinds of explanation. Hence, the plurality of sciences is grounded both on the
variety of actual beings and on the various systems of evidence.

To make matters of existence evident as matters of fact is the
purpose of all explanation. An actual being becomes a matter
of fact through information or formulation; it must find its
place in a system of evidence. When found, the actual being
is clothed in systematic garb so that it can be presented in
public. Evidence in matters of reason is simply coherence, but
in matters of fact it has other forms as well: statistical correlation, functional relativity, various measures of probability, reliability of testimony. Matters of fact are matters stated evidently. Or, to express this in reverse, existential propositions
always refer to something which is not a proposition, but is
capable of being proposed. A fact is not necessarily a deed; it
is any natural or cultural being reduced to symbolical form in a
system of evidence. Vico's famous formula, *verum est factum,*
which was proposed by him as the basic formal principle for
historical evidence, can be generalized to fit all the natural
and social sciences. Facts are made, and they are made out of
beings so related that they give evidence, clarification, ex-

planation to each other. This is the basic operation of the sciences.

Such a conception of evidence rules out self-evidence. In matters of reason there is some excuse for using the term "self-evident," since it is a desperate attempt to state what logical coherence means without trying to explain it. The basis of all explanation, we say, is self-evidently not subject to explanation. But to accept this statement as an explanation would scarcely be an example of good logic. It is at best a statement of the recognition of a logical form as a distinct kind of being. But is this recognition a kind of perception? If so, perception of what? Is it cognition? If so, where is its evidence, its credentials? Is it self-validating faith? Such questioning seems to be a beating about the bush. Nothing comes of it. Logical self-evidence, then, would appear to be a redundant formula for logical form; it explains nothing.

Let evidence, then, be accepted as a relational being or formal structure of matters which each-for-itself would not be evident, would not be a fact, but would *exist* in some other way, nontheoretically, nonevidently.

To make this ontology of science more concrete, let me call attention to the science of optics. This science is based on a natural structure, namely, the electromagnetic field in the physical world with reference to any point of view. Descriptive geometry and optics describe systems of objective relations, just as much as Euclidean geometry does. The fact that seeing beings have built-in lenses which enable them to have a visual perspective in experience, implies the more basic fact that there is systematic perspective. The correlation of perspectives is based on the existence of perspectival order. The propositions of perspective geometry which describe this order are ideas, but the order which they describe is not itself an idea but a system of relations exhibited by points of view. The radiation of light, the processes of vision, and the eyes have a structure; so do the cultural processes of visual perception and interpretation. Both the dynamics and the statics are systematic; the dynamic systems are spatio-temporal and electromagnetic whereas the static systems are purely spatial or geometric. Both kinds of beings are matters of fact for the factual sciences of biology and psychology. These sciences, too, are theoretical or formal structures; their subject matters are not. Seeing the moon, for example, is a party to all these beings. Such beings, which are candidates for becoming facts, are evidently not ideas, for ideas are not real at all if they are not related to other ideas. Their very being is in their formulation. Granted that there is this realm of ideas interrelated, the function of the factual sciences is to translate items of nature or experience into ideational structures. How they perform this function depends at least in part upon what kind of a candidate is to be formed into fact. Is it a volcanic eruption of long ago or one that is present? Is it a dream difficult to recover? Is it an emotion? Is it a war? Is it a song? These beings must first of all be named, for they do not come tagged or labeled. And the name is probably a beginning of the attempt to explain or inform the formless. These beings from the realms of nature and culture, the actual world, are not "informed matter" in the traditional sense of the Aristotelians. They are bona fide individuals of the world in action seeking entrance into the realm of facts as they appear in systematic, evidential order. This making of facts is the art in science.

Verification is one of the arts a scientist must learn, but the verities discovered must form themselves or be formulated into a system of propositions before there exists a formal cognitive structure. I would be the last person to deny that there is an element of know-how in all knowledge, but for the sake of ontological analysis I must separate in theory two kinds of being which in practice work together—the laboratory operations or methods of the scientist and the structure of his text-book or report of findings arranged not in order of discovery but in order of evidence.

EVIDENCE IN LAW

There are other arts which rely on rational structure. Take one that is closely related to the factual sciences and yet is not a science; procedure in a court of law is a distinctive type of practical discipline concerned with evidence. The principles that have been developed in the art of law to govern rules of evidence or fact-finding in court testimony constitute a well-established system in which "evidence" has a technical meaning. A law court must evaluate the mass of statements made to it by witnesses. On the basis of practical experience certain types of testimony are regarded as dubious, or inadmissible, or probably trustworthy. Here the canons of consistency or reason, though logically basic, play a subordinate role; for the difficult problems of evaluation are not mere logical problems, nor are they matters of statistical probability. They are related to the trustworthiness of kinds of witnesses, to reliability of memory to circumstantial evidence, and to other more or less psychological problems. The science of psychology is of some help here, in addition to the science of logic, but the technical rules of evidence as they develop in formal legal procedure and as they often become "mere technicalities" are systematic practical norms for practical judgment. Law exists not for knowledge but for government, and what knowledge of evidence it accepts and generates is subordinated to the practical aspects of decision or judgment. But the treatises on legal evidence are formal systems in the same sense that the sciences or cognitive systems are formal structures. They are the forms of a technique, and yet they reveal in more detail than the sciences do how difficult it is to define evidence in general.

There have been judges who have tried to present law as pure reason and themselves as mere logicians. But such attempts to reduce the art of a judge to a deductive science are now generally repudiated. Law as it is taught in law schools always involves the study of cases as well as the principles of jurisprudence. The whole complex of the academic study of law in preparation for the practice of law is occasionally referred to as "the science of law." Here "science" is Latin for "knowledge" and for the methodical learning of a profession. Any learning may be pursued in terms of "scientific method." But we must distinguish here between method or scientific, systematic learning and a science as a formal structure of generalized and integrated facts known as a body of truths. Law is not even an inductive science. It is not science at all except in the sense of being a highly formalized know-how or skilled art of settling conflicts.

FORMS IN ARTS

Skill in an art cannot be reduced to a system or a science, even though it requires the use of systems and sciences. There are no courses in any respectable college in practical experience, prudence, or wisdom. They are not subject matter or matters of fact though they can be learned; they are achievements. The possession of such an achievement implies highly disciplined habits of response, muscular control, discriminating judgment, and other virtuoso virtues; and in a sense these are structures. But they are structured movements, dynamic patterns, not formal systems in the sense in which the formulated norms of such skill can be called a formal system or body of principles. The structures with which we are now concerned are composed of the systematic relations among principles, maxims, values, standards, not the practical relations of these norms to action.

In any art the artists are convinced that there are proprieties and improprieties in the use of their media. But there is little general agreement among artists concerning what these pro-

prieties are in particular; and critics of art are quick to point out
improprieties, though they become quite dogmatic when they
attempt to construct a theory of proprieties. All are agreed that
there is such a thing as good taste in art and good judgment in
art criticism, but the formulation of why good art and good
taste are good is apt to be repudiated as pedantic and certainly
as in bad taste. No artist wants to do the proper thing, for fear
of doing what is right instead of what is good. And yet an
artist takes great pains to study his work for imperfections until
he is satisfied that it is "just right." In short, just as a moralist
analyses a situation to determine the right course of action
under the circumstances, so an artist uses his skill to construct
or compose in the proper way, given certain materials and
aims. He may have no interest in the science of proprieties, if
such a science is possible, but he nevertheless cultivates expert-
ness of judgment in his particular art.

In view of the diversity of arts and the intensity of an artist's
devotion to his art, there is even less chance for a theoretical
formulation of the principles of propriety in composition than
there is for a theory of moral decency. But the faith that
propriety has formal foundations is the same in art as in morals.

DECENCIES AND DEONTOLOGY

With this as a general account of the nature of formalities
in the arts and sciences we may be prepared to examine the
question of formal fitnesses—a bone of contention for centuries
and still a genuine problem.

In dealing with the rules of evidence or of fact-finding in court procedure, we have noted that the aim of a formal set of rules or principles is to promote greater justice of judgment on the part of judges and juries. It is scarcely necessary to point out that "justice," "judgment," "judge," and "jury" are all variations on a common theme; just judgment is good or systematic judgment based on evidence and law—the kind of judgment for which a professional judge is employed. Is it possible to generalize for all the arts the principles of good judgment? Is the achievement of the professional expert merely his possession of a skilled technique? Is it merely a methodological question, or are there existential structures involved to which we owe attention at this point in our ontology? It is easy to drift into mythology on this subject and I wish to warn of this danger and not to fall into the trap myself. My aim is to de-mythologize formal deontology, without dismissing the whole problem of deontology as antiquated metaphysics. Accordingly, I wish to inquire how much can be rescued of the traditional faiths in objective decencies, proprieties, and harmonies. These have all become terms of abuse among analysts and I am employing them consciously as such, in order to find out how much of the abuse is deserved.

There are occasional references to "public decency" even by hard-boiled realists in law and morals. But the appeal of Thomas Jefferson and other eighteenth century moralists to "a decent respect for the opinion of mankind" is now commonly regarded as an indecent subjection to popular opinion.

I have no intention of discussing here particular decencies; my only concern is: Does such a structure as decency exist? If so, is it recognized by sweeter names?

A decency or fitness, in old-fashioned terminology, is a structural element in a situation. A situation implies an existential context to which a response is required. And the ontologist argues that if a *requirement* is recognized as an objective trait of a given situation, then one or more fit responses are implied. And if all this is admitted then some deontological category is a necessary requirement of ontology. What shall it be called, if a new name is needed, and how shall it be conceived to be?

An adequate, satisfactory response to a requirement is nothing extraordinary and fits into the general context of values, which we have analyzed before. But the kind of requirement to which a decency is a response is not made by a person or another living being in terms of its needs, as is the case in a value situation. In the deontological situation the situation as a dynamic whole makes the requirement; and it is someone who understands the whole situation, whether he be party to it or not, who judges what is the suitable thing to be done under the circumstances. The kind of "ought to be" involved here is merely the completion of an existent situation which is determinative or demanding, so that the "ought" appears to be already contained in what is there. What is there, in other words, has already decided what is-to-be.

That there are situations of this kind seems undeniable. The real question is to what extent this kind of demanding situation is at the bottom of right and wrong in general. Human beings make claims on each other and expect certain types of reciprocity. But is there any reason for such behavior beyond the traits of human nature or the establishments of human cultures? Is right and wrong based on approvals and disapprovals or is there a norm to guide approving and disapproving, that is structurally determined by the circumstances in which men find themselves? Is there a way of determining decent and indecent attitudes and action by an analysis of typical situations, instead of by an analysis of actual conduct? And if so, can such norms be generalized and systematized?

If the problem of decent conduct were similar to the problem of the right move to make in chess, given a certain distribution of pieces, there would be a formal structure and knowledge of right and wrong. It is the aim of deontological moralists to prove that the right move morally speaking can be calculated analogously to calculations in the theory of chess. This kind of analytical ethics is quite different from Bentham's utilitarian calculus of pleasures and pains, though Bentham called his ethics a deontology. For this is not a prudential calculus in a generalized science of happiness, it is an information theory for a science of obligation. If an objective or situational calculus of what-needs-to-be-done can be generalized or systematized, a formal science of duty is possible, which is neither a theory of values nor a theory of categorical right and wrong in the sense that the right or decent could not be reduced to other terms. In one sense, this reduces social relations to a game whose rules can be discovered, but it does not imply gambling on probabilities.

Far be it from me to build a moral computer, but I suggest that such a model for a science of decency is not absurd. Like Bentham's calculus, it may have no practical value for legislation, but it at least provides a theoretical model for deontology as an aspect of ontology. The French existentialists have celebrated man's being *engagé* in general. Such preaching could be interpreted as a faith in deontology, but it would be unfair to interpret existentialist analyses of situational determinism in terms of decency, when they are intended to serve the knowledge of absurdity. In one sense, playing chess is futile, but it is not absurd. Similarly the study of the right moves in social relations may be an unprofitable study, but it is not irrational. The chief difference between morality and chess is that in chess one begins with given rules, whereas in moral relations one begins with given obstacles and tries to discover the rules of the game.

Let me illustrate this general problem of deontological structure by referring to a situation which combines the perspectives of morals and art. A person dies; the body must be disposed of. The person has friends; if not, there is at least a community of neighbors for whom the decent disposition of the body is an urgent, practical problem. Here is a common situation which obviously calls for decencies and proprieties. Burial rites are among the oldest of human formalities. The practical problem is complicated because it is almost never conceived merely in terms of propriety and decency. A "decent burial" is usually perverted by consideration of financial display as a symbol of affection or honor, or by institutional exploitation of the mourners by "undertakers" (a curious word), by preachers, by publicity. Leaving aside all these additional features of the funeral situation as it exists in various cultures, there is a minimum, essential predicament of giving an appropriate burial to the corpse of a person. It is pathetic to study the ingenious ways in which principles of decency and propriety are violated on such occasions. The situation is so universal that one might expect better formalities for such occasions. Memorial arts are relatively primitive and often shocking to those most directly involved. The formalization is usually excessive and artificial, but the need for formal expression, in view of the universal elements in the situation, is always in the foreground. Moralizing seems indecent and artistic display improper. I know of no better evidence for the recognition of an objective formalized propriety than this mortuary situation. For here formal propriety is at a premium, demanded but seldom discovered.

RELIGIOUS FORMALISM

This leads me to suggest a consideration of the art of celebration in general from the point of view of occasions which by their nature demand a decent expression. Misplaced formalities, as in politics, diplomacy, law, and learning, are bad enough, but miserable formalities when formality is appropriate are worse. There are occasions, like the situation created by a death in a circle of friends, that obviously need celebration of some kind: victories, births, marriages, graduations, vacations, remorse, despair, crises in general, demand an art of celebration, consecration, commiseration, or congratulation, as the case may be. There is an ancient saying, both profound and pathetic, that if tomorrow we die, today we ought to celebrate! All the arts, and many vices, lend themselves to the need for celebration.

But it is religion that has a primary and professional concern in a large range of formalized celebration. Among its achievements should be the fine art of celebration, and it is common knowledge that when the other arts seem inadequate for the formalization of an extraordinary occasion, religious ceremonies are called in to meet the needs. Whatever else religion does, it formalizes formality. To do this well, appropriately, honestly, is a very fine art, and in its prime the religious art has called all the other arts to its aid. But formality is easily carried to deficiency or excess, celebration being a more enjoyable indulgence than labor. During the Middle Ages, the governments that were concerned for the economic prosperity of the people had to interfere continually with the church's multiplication of holy days, especially during harvest.

This discussion raises the whole issue of the relation of good form to formality. They are frequently incompatible. However, the pervasive interest in both throughout human cultures is evidence of man's search for formal proprieties and his creation of artificial formalities when he does not find things decent as they are.

HARMONIES

Harmonies are out of fashion, I know, in this world of dissonances, but I ought to make at least a passing bow to them for what they are. What can I say about objective compatibilities?

I am referring now not to the unisons of reason, logic, mathematics, and theoretical systems, but to those proportions that show themselves in other beings. Ratios and proportions that are discovered in the world by man and that render things commensurate either by counting or by analogy are among the most ancient and famous forms of being. But despite the conviction that strife rules all things, it was difficult before Darwin to erect this chaotic realm of conflict to the level of a formal structure. Tragedy, which has long been regarded as a significant structure in existence, has usually been interpreted as the child of necessity rather than of strife. To see in conflict itself a form or structure is a relatively recent achievement.

The structures that have been most cherished and dignified as having "being" are composed of compatible elements combined in proportions. Proportionality pervades all formal structures of sciences and all compositions of the arts, of morals and philosophies. And it was assumed that proportions received their culminating forms in mathematics and music. These two were regarded until recently as inherently devoted to exploring harmonies. Today the conceptions of mathematical and musical orders have been expanded to such an extent that the conception of harmony no longer does them justice. Ratios and proportions are still basic, but harmonious structure has taken a subordinate place. Just as *concordia* still receives lip service, so harmony still has a sweet sound. But the inventions of modern reason, mathematics, and arts have made competitive co-existence a much more prevalent pattern for the analysis of formal structures. The crisscross of vibrations in the atmosphere, the variety of rays pouring onto the earth from what is sometimes still called "outer" space, the complexity of rhythms, moods, coexistences, in human society have accustomed us to conceive as order what former generations would have perceived as chaos.

Above all, we have at last been compelled to think of our world of forms in pluralistic terms. We hardly even dream of a universal structure or form of forms. The information of things is relational, relative, multidimensional. And as for harmonies, they are all the more precious because more rare.

I suspect that I shall be accused in all this deontological speculation of skating out imprudently onto the thin ice of natural law doctrine. Hence it may be useful to close with a few critical comments on the relation of this defense of structural propriety to the theories of natural law in ethics and jurisprudence. Already in the course of these lectures I have referred to natural law concepts as mythological, literally false but symbolically significant. My first objection, then, to natural law theory is that I do not believe that deontological structures can be located either in the general order of nature, if it exists, or in the structure of human nature. Here I think I am following Woodbridge, admitting teleology and values into the analysis of organic processes without admitting that nature has a moral dimension. Nature can be as "neutral" as Woodbridge claimed it to be in relation to man's pursuit of happiness. This is man's affair and is not dictated either by natural laws or by human nature's drives. It is an operation, probably the fundamental operation of man; and whenever it succeeds it is a triumph of human art and intelligence. The Stoics were and still are wrong when they conceive morality as "living according to nature."

However, despite nature's neutrality, man's cultural environment and conditioning are such that his moral field, that is, the very structure of his situations, is frequently determining for his movements and decisions. I do not say that this is always so. The idea that the moral life is an exercise of freedom or self-control has been greatly exaggerated, especially by those who, still under the spell of Kant and neo-Kantians, have erected a categorical curtain between facts and values, between the "is" and the "ought," between ontology and the normative sciences. There are more laws in the world than nature's, and no science is merely natural. Whatever may be the truth about the pursuit of happiness, a pursuit which has not as yet been reduced to a science, and which is certainly not a problem in ontological science, the experience of obligations and responsibilities is certainly, as Spinoza said, a form of human bondage to the world and to mankind. Human beings find themselves, whether because they are cast or thrown or grown into their world, in situations or environments which make demands on them objectively, peremptorily, and impersonally. They are categorical but not imperatives; neither are they natural necessities; but they are inescapable compulsions. Duties come to us from the outside; they are external, but not on that account natural. They are cultural powers which gradually eat their wormy way into the very core of our consciences. They begin by being institutional and end by being very personal. Similarly, there are structural factors in the practical problems of any composer, painter, surgeon, judge, statesman, or farmer that dictate certain moves or requirements of their crafts. In the cases of the farmer and the surgeon, the craftsman may feel that he is being controlled by natural powers, but even these crafts are controlled in part by many kinds of institutional requirements and instruments. There are exigencies and obligations in human experience which, though not cases of natural law, are creations of a particular world situation or local circumstance that compels attention and satisfaction. To dismiss such situations from moral science as emergencies and to seek an *ad hoc* shelter until the storms of crisis blow over and normalcy is restored are now recognized as morally irresponsible attitudes and intellectually complacent dogmatism. No human determinations are ever purely external or purely internal, wholly fated or wholly free. It is therefore an important task of ontological analysis to do justice to the existence of demands arising from situational structures.

If the ontological aspects of proprieties are recognized, I have no special attachment to the term "deontology." But it seems important to detach this analysis from the confusions and irrelevancies of the polemics about "natural law," "functionalism," "value determination," and "organicism," with which this problem is now overburdened. The application of situational explanation and conditioning to cultural structures and human experience does not require a distinctive type of explanation, for such analyses are commonplaces of physical, biological, and social sciences and can readily be distinguished from teleology in the sense of John Stuart Mill's "canon of ends" or Kant's "kingdom of ends" as a basis for deductive moral science. I am not suggesting a new type of knowledge or causation or explanation, but rather a particular form of "objective relativism" in a realistic survey of systems and of formal being.

V. THE WORLD OF BEINGS

We have talked of many things and asked them how they are. Though few of them can answer, they at least throw enough light on each other so that we can try to tell them what they are and how they are related to each other. Why they are as they are, who knows? Most beings might be satisfied with this information, but we philosophers are unable to let the matter rest at that. For when this information gives us a clue to why some things are what they are, and when we can explain to whom it may concern why these things are related as they are, we begin to hope that our analytical inventory might turn into an ontological science. If we could explain in each case why a thing is, we imagine that we ought to explain why there is anything. Why all this picking the world to pieces if in the end the world is unintelligible? Analysis is not an end in itself: the aim is to understand the world of beings as if the world itself were a being.

There is a wise old verse in the *Panchatantra* of India which I might paraphrase freely but not loosely as follows:

> Do not grasp the universe
> Unless you really can.

The popcorn hopping up and down
Will crack no frying pan.

Is this the last word of practical wisdom? Are all things in their vain poppings and hoppings, their combustions and explosions, caught between the impenetrable dome of heaven above and the heat of hell around and below?

Sages have toyed with such analogies and images for ages. They exploit the factual unintelligibility of the world as a whole for preaching sermons and giving morality plays. It would be a sad ending indeed if our ontologizing led us, too, into such moralizing. On the contrary, I have done my little best to explain as rationally as anything can be explained that the world of beings could not be as if it were one of them. Our term "world" does not name an individual nor a class nor a total. It denotes the ontological ultimate but it does not explain itself. We must let the world be *the* world and not *a* world. Logically, of course, we can speak of possible worlds as if they might be. But such talk is vain ontologically. It throws light neither on being nor on nonbeing. Let us leave the world as it is—alone. In other words, let things be in the world as they actually are, without asking wherein the world may have its being.

The unintelligibility of the world as a whole means that there is no idea or concept of the structure of the world. The astronomical universe, is, as we have agreed, only a part, an enormous part, of the world about which we are speaking. Even if astronomers can make all the stars intelligible, the world is still not a unity. The popular phrase for the world as *englo-bant non englobé,* encompassing without being encompassed, is useful as a designation but not as a definition. Lacking a reliable idea of what the world is "in and for itself," men may nevertheless conceive the world in its functioning as the human environment.

"The world is always the world of him who speaks of it. The Ptolemaic character of thought cannot be overcome by any astronomical Copernicanism. . . . Any perspective is always relative to the being who generates it. . . . None of these worlds is ever given; to exist they must be constructed."[1]

This states succinctly what I call a person's *appropriation* of the world, constructing its order in terms of its functioning as his environment. And it is obviously impossible to get an idea of the world as it is by trying to sum up these appropriations. If any idea of the totality of existences is always in such perspective, it is meaningless to summarize such ideas in order to get what Kant called "an absolute totality of the basic idea of existing things" (*absolute Totalität des Inbegriffs existierender Dinge*). However, it is important to note that all such constructions take place *within* the "given" world, and it is this given, unordered, world that is the real world. It is not true that the world is *only* the world in perspective, humanly constructed to order. Everyone knows that mankind is a latecomer in the

1 Translated from Augusto Guzzo, "Le concept philosophique de monde," *Dialectica,* 57-58, XV (1961) pp. 105-6.

world and therefore the world must have been, even if it should not be now, quite independent of human perspective. All such discussion of how the world really exists seems futile, beyond the observation that its known structures are all in perspective. Men can dream as they please of "the world order"; meanwhile all discoveries are made within the varied fields of the world, and they do not compose a totality in any intelligible sense. What I have called the togetherness of the dimensions in the world, or what the phenomenologists call *Sinnzusammenhänge,* must be accepted as gifts, not as human creations. The world is not made *tout par tout*[2] for all the creations of all are still in the world, of whose creation we indwellers are ignorant.

Within the world there remain, according to our analysis, nature, culture, and structure, these three, but greater than these is their togetherness in the world. What may well amaze us is the fact that despite all the systems and structures which we discover in the world there is no evidence that they all are parts of a single system. Systems bind individuals together and then in turn individual systems are bound together in more inclusive systems. But as we follow the diversified ways in which things and systems are together we do not arrive at a total system. Totality is a purely denotative term and implies no systematic structure. For even though our efforts to relate all to all may succeed, the relations do not form a systematic unity. There is no totalizing process, no summing up of commensurables. The world is not a sum of beings but a receptacle

2 *Ibid.,* p. 126.

in which diverse beings mingle in an indescribable compatibility. We have no ground for saying that beings could not possibly constitute a systematic unity; all we can say is that they actually do not, to the best of our knowledge. Therefore, wishing future ontologists all the luck in the world, I must report that my own attempt at ontology turns out not to be a system, and this is due, I believe, not to my love of pluralism, which is by no means passionate, but simply to *natura rerum*— the way things happen to be, naturally, culturally, and formally.

Where does this leave us? Nature, culture, and structure are not distinct beings. Anything in the world is apt to be involved directly or indirectly in all three modes of being; of this we have given many illustrations. And yet such three dimensional being is not completely systematic because the so-called dimensions cannot be correlated analytically and are therefore "dimensions" only metaphorically or practically.

If this trinity is not triune, could it perhaps be commune? Could the world be a trinitarian community, as certain theologians have held the Holy Trinity to be? Examine a community within the world, New York, for example. Take the Museum of Natural History and combine it with the Metropolitan Museum of Art. Would putting them under one roof bring them closer together in any other sense? Let us add also the Metropolitan Opera and City Hall, and Wall Street, and Columbia University, and a few other universities; then the Bronx, zoo and all; and the theaters, subways, tunnels, bridges, wires, television sets, and all the rest. The total would make our familiar New York community. This is a real individual being but far from being a unified system, as the New York Edison Company is, in whose power we all are. Community or social unity is a distinct kind of togetherness of many very different beings. Cosmologists, Whitehead for example, have modeled the world on such community, less than systematic structure, less than organic, but at least a network of communication systems.

Our trinitarian analysis, however, yields no such picture. In fact, it yields no picture at all. All things together are in the world, but not in communication, and consequently the togetherness is not describable in general, not even sentimentally. It seems best, therefore, not to capitalize Being, as respectful ontologists still do. There is no such thing except in the world of the imagination.

At this world of imagined being we must take a last look. Even it is within the world of which we have been speaking and because it is there the world is more complicated and unstable. If imaginary beings and ghosts were really "dead and gone" from the very "sphere and room of being" our world would be very different from what it is. These imaginary beings readily become foci of attachment for groups of real beings and complicate their real relations. They may be great sources of energy —bewildering, enticing, tempting, and also organizing, directing movements in all directions. Many movements of masses are due to other things besides other masses. And when movements are thus directed it is impossible to fit them all into any one system or community. For the world of the imagination is notoriously free and chaotic, and the whole world, having acquired this free-wheeling dimension is subject to change without notice; it has a genuine future.

There is another school of cosmologists who believe that there are levels or stages of being. Most important in recent times are those who have constructed an order of dependency among kinds of beings. There is nothing on which nature depends; this follows by definition, since nature is that automaton out of which all things are generated. At the terra firma bottom of dependable beings, therefore, they place physical processes. Living beings are dependent on other, nonliving processes, which are independent of life. Conscious beings are dependent on organic or living beings, not vice versa. Intelligent beings are dependent on conscious life, cultural being on mental being, and so on. Nicolai Hartmann's scheme of the strata in the real world will serve well to illustrate this ontology of emergent evolution.

Hartmann's world can be represented as a kind of wedding cake: the bottom layer of inorganic being is extensive but not very thick; built upon it, is a thicker but less extensive layer of organic or living beings; next comes a layer, still thicker but smaller, of sensitive or conscious living beings; and on top of all is a slender, towering layer of illuminated, sugar-coated being called mind, spirit, or *Geist*. Holding these layers together is a "law" or principle of "one-over-another" (*Ueber-*

bauung) which implies that on top of a part (never the whole extent) of a layer there is a superstructure in which some of the categories of the lower structure reappear in a new context of new categories, so that there is always a categorial filling which two layers have in common and which holds them together. The filling between other layers is a different filling. And even though there may be a bit of common sugar or egg in all, the categories which emerge through all layers are so transformed by their new contexts that they have different functions. Let me read a rough translation of Hartmann's own summary of how the world hangs together in layers despite the fact that, as he admits, "it is impossible to give a general formula for the properties which enable a category to rise into higher layers."[3]

The distance that separates strata of beings when a new group of categories appears suddenly on a new level is not to be thought of as an empty space but as a qualitative differentiation of structures one above another. . . . There is a special categorial principle in addition to the principles of distinct levels and of their interdependence (the higher on the lower) which constitutes a third structural characteristic of the whole order of being. We can call this third group of principles "the laws of coherence" for they describe the context of the categories of any level. They can be formulated in two sentences: (1) The categories of a level of being constitute a closed system in which they together (not singly) determine the patterns of their level. (2) They imply each other internally as well, so that when one of them appears the others are necessarily involved. Such contextual unity does not exist between levels. And when some of the categories

3 Translated from Nicolai Hartmann, *Neue Wege der Ontologie*. (Stuttgart; Kohlhammer, 1947) p. 257.

ascend to higher levels they participate in the coherence structure of that higher level. This is the explanation of the fact that the levels are clearly distinct, but they are distinct only in the categorial sense. Hence, too, the law of distance between levels agrees very well with the thorough continuity of forms. And if the unity of the world were to exhibit such a continuity, it would not be contrary to the laws of levels and dependence. Whether this is actually the case, our categorial analysis is unable to tell.[4]

In other words, the process of emergence of world levels implies the symbolization of the formalization of the finalization of mechanical being. At each step in this process the categories themselves are transformed rather than integrated. Even the distinction between possibility and actuality is different for different levels. If this is the case, dependence itself means a different relation at different stages, and the whole order-of-levels in the world is inexplicable in terms of any one kind of explanation.

This is a curious kind of unity for the world, but it is in general a true account of the complicated relations within *human* existence. In short, this kind of ontology, which culminates in a cosmology, seems to be little more than a transcription on a world-wide scale of the varied aspects of *human* being, arranged in the conventional hierarchy of matter, life, soul and spirit. Such an ontologized anthropology is a product of philosophical heavy industry, but it explains nothing, and leaves the world a bit more complicated than it need be. It also leaves ontology more anthropomorphic than it ought to be. Human being is

4 ibid., pp. 282-83.

the most interesting kind of being even for an ontologist, but this interest should not warp cosmological theory. The levels or strata and the hierarchy of being constructed out of them are appropriate enough in the context of human nature, but when they become elements of world structure and cosmic evolution, they are all too human.

It behooves ontology to be very modest about reporting the structure of the world, especially in terms of top-and-bottom. Cultural being, from the point of view of human ontologists must be almost wholly a matter of human being. For though they must admit the possibility and even probability of other cultures on other planets and in other galaxies, there is nothing to be said about them, nor do they throw light on human prejudices so long as they remain unknown. It is therefore impossible to estimate the extent and varieties of cultural being in the physical universe or natural world. All we know is that human culture is of no astronomical magnitude and that human evolution is no measure of universal evolution, if there should be such a process. Ontology is a human concern but all human concerns are probably negligible in the world as a whole, if it is a whole.

Another common attempt to give being added dignity is to add together nature and culture, calling their sum "actuality," then to add on to actuality the realm of formality, calling the grand total "reality." There is no law against such mathematics, but there is the danger that the inventors of reality imagine that they have found something more than the world. Whether it adds up to more or not, reality is more subject to worship than is the world. Therefore philosophers who disdain the "primitive" cults of the cosmos, yet maintain that it is less idolatrous to deify reality. Anyone who takes reality realistically would appear to lack a sense of humor if he worshipped it. But reality is readily idealized, more easily than the world can be, and such idealizations, which are evidently monstrous follies and superstitions, still pass for "high religion."

The celebration of Being has obsessed both secular and religious minds. There was a time in the history of mythology and ontology when such celebration appeared to be appropriate. Possibly it is still appropriate. But in view of the deterioration in both being and its celebration, it seems to me absurd, inappropriate, idolatrous, and empty form to bow the knee to Being. Being should not be capitalized in the first place, not even in German. While there was a cosmos, there was some ground for a cosmopolitan cultus. But with the cosmos gone out of being, it is very difficult to give formal expression to such celebration. Surely the metaphysicians take the Lord's name in vain when they deify Being, and the existentialists do worse, when they magnify what they no longer glorify.

Santayana, shortly before leaving the world of the living, wrote: "To ignore the world is ignominious and practically dangerous, because unless you understand and respect things foreign, you will never perceive the special character of things at home or of your own mind."[5] For a foreigner like Santayana

5 George Santayana, *My Host the World* (New York; Scribners, 1953) p. 35.

this may be a good reason for respecting the world, and as a general warning against provincialism it is wholesome advice. But even if one feels at home in the world, it is good sense to perceive the "special character" of human affairs in the context of the world without ever "understanding" the whole world. It takes little more than an understanding of how close human beings are to that monstrous furnace, the sun, to instil in them a distant respect for such hellish fire.

Reality by any other name is respectable and will prevail, whatever happens to mankind. But it is easy to confuse such existential primacy and priority with the doctrine that "truth will prevail" or that human values are everlasting. The things that man should hold sacred may have little or nothing to do with any ultimate destiny of man in the world or of the world itself. The real is the measure of illusions and has priority over them, but the real is also the measure of true sentences and has priority over truth. This omnicompetence of the real, however, should not receive such titles as either God or "brute" fact. Facticity, to use the French term, is a poor object of worship and an inappropriate object of scorn. The world does not ask to be accepted any more than God asked Adam and Eve to worship their creator. There is a human decency in a civilized respect for paternity, but the world, the real world, is far from being a heavenly father. There is no doubt something awesome and awe-inspiring about finding oneself in the real world; it is more intelligent to stand in wonder at it than to try to explain it or to escape it. But all these questions of how human beings should behave in the face of the world are questions of morals and manners, not of reality.

The unity of the world is exhibited here and now, and it is not a structural unity. It cannot be told, it must be admitted, for it precedes all analysis. To derive the knowledge of the world's unity from the results of analysis is as vain as the task of restoring Humpty Dumpty, or the raising of the dead. Things are as they are in the world and not as they are methodically known to be. Knowledge of being is always *ex post facto*.

The chief obstacle to a realistic ontology is the presupposition that we arrive at reality ultimately, not in the temporal sense of arriving at the last days of the world, but in the cognitive sense of arriving in the last analysis. Our ontology, on the contrary, must begin with reality, for there is nothing more ultimate than the immediate, and this we learn "in the last analysis." The ultimate is usually represented as the unconditional, and the unconditional is represented as the metaphysical ground of freedom. For the mystics and the dialecticians this unconditional "abyss" of being lies at the end of the mind's journey through conditioned existence. But analysis has no such end, for in the last analysis the conditional nature of being is more conspicuous than ever. The unconditioned ultimate is found, if anywhere, in the immediate. *Das Unbedingte ist das Unmittelbare.*

The immediate in experience is, of course, not unconditional in nature; it is always a phase in a process. It is experience

robbed of its meaning in an operation and taken as sheer presence of process—pure *Dasein*. This involves an act of abstraction and of violence to normal consciousness. It is emotion
robbed of its natural context as motivation and of its empirical
context as intelligence. Such passive awareness of feeling is an
aspect of the psychophysics of action; it is an extrapolation of
meaning from all reference and of consciousness from all concerns. But it is not momentary, for presence is always duration,
and abstract presence is endurance or encounter without
thought. Ernest Hocking relates a curious (but typical) remark
by Whitehead, who in discussing process, said: "Reality is becoming; it is passing before one—a remark too obvious to make
. . . You can't catch a moment by the scruff of the neck— it's
gone, you know." [6] Such an attempt to conceive the immediate presence instantaneously is countered by Hocking, when
he refers in his comment on this remark to "the immediate
experience of common humanity." This comes closer to an
intelligible concept of the immediate but it leaves the important term "common humanity" undefined. I would interpret this to mean that immediacy, though private, is an
everyday fact of human living, though only philosophers may
abstract it from its context of daily affairs. Even if we take our
being-present carelessly, in passing, it is not the present that
passes, but the cares and concerns of normal consciousness, by
which the present is further extended into past and future.

6 William E. Hocking, "Whitehead as I knew him," in *Journal of Philosophy*,
LVIII, 505 (Sept. 14, 1961).

Taking the world as it comes to us, without questioning, with its immediate content of joy or sorrow, routine or frustration, is "common" enough among mankind, and ontologists must take seriously such living as both the starting point and ultimate reference of being reflective. The present, which has arrived and is in that sense an end of becoming, is at the same time the beginning of what-is-to-be; it is where past and future meet, not momentarily but continually. Any one who is fond of Greek can call it the Alpha and Omega of reality, if this makes it more ultimate to him. But "common humanity" is apt to accept it without this classical christening.

Reality is the subject-given as well as the object-to-be-known of ontological analysis, and to imagine that there is a wide gulf between the world whence our questioning arises and the reality which we learn to know is to make an assumption designed to be frustrating. In other words, the concepts of the unconditional and of the immediate are both abstractions. Reality is not a succession of pure immediacies held in chains by the all-encompassing world, nor is it a final, super-worldly resting place for minds at their wits' end. If reality is real it must be identical with the world in which both bodies and minds work together. But the truth about this world is less real, for it exists only in fragments and varying perspectives; in its ideal form or perfection it does not exist at all.

Because the theory of the real is so confused, it seems prudent to try to get along without it. Let the world be made of nature, culture, and structure in varied combinations, and let this be all that analysis can do to make the ways of the world more intelligible. If they need to be made more real, we might do well to go outdoors and let our encounters enlighten our lectures. But this is no argument against a decent, analytical ontology; it is against the ontological argument, to be sure, but we have already bypassed that argument.

In short, being is no fit object of criticism or praise, and hence, the only useful kind of ontology is analytic, tentative, piecemeal. Being does not come to us in pieces; we must pick it to pieces carefully, learning as we go along how we got the pieces and knowing that when we put the pieces together we have in our hands not being but ontology, and ontology of all things is always subject to criticism.

EPILOGUE

Among the omissions for which this ontology will be criticised is my failure to deal with non-being. How is it not-to-be? What factual relations are there between what is and what is not?

Logically, being and non-being are opposites or "negate" each other, *when used as predicates*. In themselves they neither affirm or deny. But in this "subject-object world of language," as it is sometimes called, a particular frame of reference is either stated or understood. Usually the reference is to a particular kind of being or field of beings; when ontologists refer to any or all kinds of being, while saying something about an absolute nul class, as for example, "There is no non-being," their sentence is either a tautology or is meaningless. Just as "A is non-B" does not imply the existence of A, so the use of non-B as a predicate does not imply the existence of non-B, except as a predicate.

And this leads to the more practical question. The real problems of non-being concern the exclusion of something from a particular way of being. "A is absent" or "A is missing" or some other reference to what Aristotle called facts of "privation" are not references to non-beings, but to not-being-where-wanted-or-expected. So too, being dead is a state of being, not of non-being. Suppose someone wants to know, "Are there two ways to town?" The answer would not be "Yes, the ways are two," but "Yes, there are two ways" or "No, there is only one way." In this last case the classical dialecticians would assert that, because there is a missing way, there is a positive being of a non-being (so-called negative fact). I used to work with an Irish carpenter who, when inspecting a barn for repairs, would look at the sagging ridge and say, "See? There's a goneness there." Gonenesses in barns and college classes are familiar acquaintances. But even admitting with the gloomy brand of existentialists that all temporal beings are headed for "goneness", I see no scientific reason for transforming this situation into a dialectical luxury.

The world, by definition, does not imply the being of something beyond it. If, then, we speak of God or some other being transcending the world and having a kind of being which is foreign to "worldly existence," we are changing our definition of "world" and "being." It is possible to speak of God or some other being as not *in* the world, but *of* the world, in a significant sense. Thus we might speak of "the cause of the world," without implying that the world is actually in causal relation to something beyond it. But such talk would not contribute information about the world, its cause, or the realm of non-being. If some day we are able to explain more about the world's being than we can at present, the meaning of "world" would be expanded. It would not imply that a non-being has come into being.

The limitations of language readily create paradoxes, contradictions, and puzzles out of the reference to "non-being." That "non-being" is a term of discourse is a truism. Beyond this, however, the less said about non-being, the better. For to talk about nothing, besides being idle, is not a linguistic necessity in any reasonably adequate language.